TRADING MIND

WHERE BRAIN MEETS PROFITS

PRANAM GHAGARE

CONTENTS

CHAPTER 1

INTRODUCTION

Trading is a journey that entices many with the temptation of quick money, but experienced traders are aware of the harsh truth, the stock market is arguably the most difficult place to find easy money. A solid strategy that changes over time and controls emotions in each trade is necessary for success. To maximize profits and minimize losses in the presence of high trading and impact costs, you should have control over greed, fear, and pride. There are similarities between trading and business. There are countless restaurant closures for every successful one. In the same way, hundreds of traders fail for every successful one. Trading has a low entry barrier, unlike starting a business, which demands extensive effort. Trading is not just about learning technical analysis, it is about understanding yourself and becoming better at handling the challenges throughout your trading journey.

The neglected aspect? *Trading Psychology*.

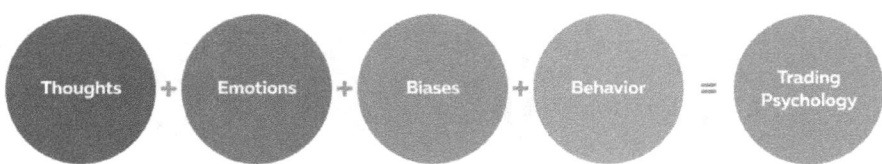

It is just as important to understand thoughts, emotions, biases, and behaviors in human psychology as it is in numbers and charts.

We will explore the important role of psychology in navigating the complexities of trading. The goal of this book is not just to emphasize the importance of trading psychology but also to guide you through a series of connected chapters and practical steps, helping you build a strong mental foundation for successful trading.

Trading Psychology:

"Cut your losses and celebrate your profits" is the motto of almost every profitable trader. It seems simple, doesn't it? However, trading is an all-consuming profession and career choice, as any trader will tell you. You will discover that it is difficult to keep your emotions apart from your trading decisions, whether it is because you want to increase your income or it is your passion. However, a seasoned trader is also aware that it is never a good idea to allow emotions to cloud your judgment when making trading decisions, this is called *Trading Psychology.*

Each trader has a different set of characteristics and psychological tendencies that shape their approach to trading. This is referred to as your *"trader DNA."* Understanding your trading DNA is crucial in adapting a trading strategy that fits your skills and limitations. Although it can be challenging to analyze yourself to recognize and address undesirable and ineffective personality qualities, these characteristics frequently make us struggle in the market.

For instance, someone who is stubborn in their daily life might hold onto losing positions for a longer period in the hopes of an unlikely turnaround. Your trading account could suffer substantial damage as a result of this unwillingness to accept losses.

Let's say there are two traders: **Harsh** and **Shubham**.

Shubham: An extremely sensitive individual with a high emotional quotient.

Harsh: A person who is less sensitive to his feelings and has a low emotional quotient.

If we assign Harsh and Shubham the same profitable trading strategy, what do you suppose each of them would have as an annual return?

Here are your options:

1. **Harsh will be surpassed by Shubham.**
2. **Harsh is going to beat Shubham.**
3. **The returns will be the same for them.**

Most would believe that the strategies should yield the same returns because they are the same.

However, "Harsh will outperform Shubham both financially and emotionally" is the accurate response.

The Reason:

The emotions we experience following a win or a loss cause us to make illogical choices. These illogical choices result in more losses as well as an upsurge of emotions. Until the account blows up, the cycle keeps going.

This is most likely the reason algorithmic traders have gained so much traction in the last ten years alone, they exclude human emotion from the picture. When a streak of losses occurs, many retail traders tend to blame the strategy, although what should be blamed is their *Trading Psychology*.

The following pie chart summarises how important strategy, risk management, and trading psychology are to creating a profitable trading system.

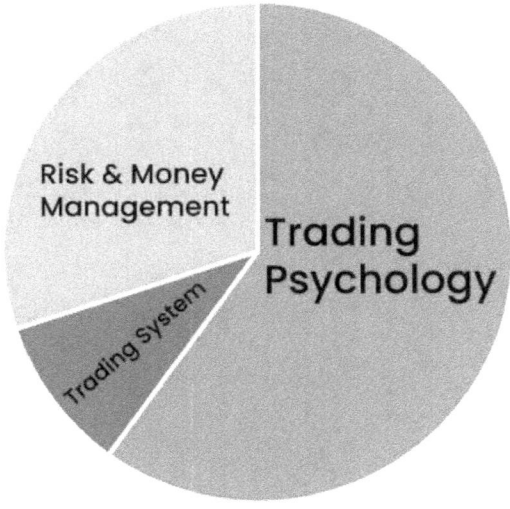

Successful Trading

According to a study from Van K Tharp, a New York Times best-selling author of Super Trader, our psychology plays the largest role in our success as a trader, as the pie chart above tells us, our success in trading depends 60% on Psychology, 30% on Risk Management, and only 10% on your Trading Strategy.

Each chapter in this book is a building block toward creating and maintaining the ultimate trading mindset. Step-by-step, you will create a solid framework for trading success, making sure your mental foundation is as strong as your technical skills. This book is not just about theories, it is a practical toolkit. In the upcoming chapters, expect clear, doable steps, and plans to manage risks, build confidence, and reflect on your trading. The real value is not just in learning, but in doing.

CHAPTER 2

ASSESSMENT QUIZ

Welcome to the self-assessment quiz designed to help you gain insights into your current trading mindset. As you answer each question, be honest with yourself. Let us get started!

1. Emotional Awareness:

How often do your emotions impact your trading decisions?

A. Rarely (4 points)

B. Occasionally (3 points)

C. Frequently (2 points)

D. Always (1 point)

Example: Imagine a recent losing trade. If you stayed calm and rational, you might choose 'A'. If emotions influenced your decisions, you might lean towards 'C' or 'D'.

2. Risk Perception:

How comfortable are you with taking calculated risks in your trades?

A. Very comfortable (4 points)

B. Somewhat comfortable (3 points)

C. Neutral (2 points)

D. Uncomfortable (1 point)

Example: Consider a scenario where you decide to enter a trade with a stoploss. If you feel confident in your decision, 'A' is suitable. If you hesitate due to potential risks, 'D' may be more accurate.

3. Patience and Discipline:

How would you rate your level of patience and discipline during a losing streak?

A. Extremely patient and disciplined (4 points)

B. Moderately patient and disciplined (3 points)

C. Struggling with patience and discipline (2 points)

D. Impulsive and undisciplined (1 point)

Example: Reflect on how you handled a recent losing streak. If you stuck to your plan and remained patient, 'A' fits. If you deviate impulsively and go searching for some other strategy, you might choose 'D'.

4. Goal Clarity:

Do you have clear short-term and long-term trading goals?

A. Yes, both short-term and long-term goals are well-defined (4 points)

B. Somewhat clear, but could use more specificity (3 points)

C. Uncertain about goals (2 points)

D. No clear goals established (1 point)

Example: Consider your trading goals. If you have specific, achievable goals, 'A' is suitable. If your goals are vague or unclear, you might lean towards 'C' or 'D'.

5. Learning and Adaptation:

How open are you to learning from both successful and unsuccessful trades?

A. Very open to learning (4 points)

B. Open, but room for improvement (3 points)

C. Reluctant to learn from mistakes (2 points)

D. Not interested in analyzing trades (1 point)

Example: Think about your reaction after a recent trade. If you actively seek lessons, 'A' is fitting. If you avoid reflecting on mistakes, 'D' may be more accurate.

6. Routine and Preparedness:

How consistent are you with following a pre-trade routine and being prepared for market changes?

A. Extremely consistent (4 points)

B. Fairly consistent (3 points)

C. Inconsistent (2 points)

D. No pre-trade routine established (1 point)

Example: Evaluate your preparation before a trade. If you have a consistent routine, 'A' is appropriate. If your approach lacks consistency, you might lean towards 'C' or 'D'.

7. External Influences:

To what extent do external factors, such as market news or social media, influence your trading decisions?

A. Rarely influenced (4 points)

B. Occasionally influenced (3 points)

C. Often influenced (2 points)

D. Heavily influenced (1 point)

Example: Think about a recent trade decision. If external factors had minimal impact, 'A' is suitable. If you often rely on external cues, 'D' may be more accurate.

8. Reflection and Journaling:

Do you maintain a trading journal to reflect on your trades, decisions, and emotions?

A. Regularly journal and reflect (4 points)

B. Occasionally journal (3 points)

C. Rarely journal (2 points)

D. Do not maintain a trading journal (1 point)

Example: Reflect on your journaling habits. If you consistently journal, 'A' is fitting. If you seldom document your experiences, 'C' or 'D' may be accurate.

9. Adaptability to Market Changes:

How comfortable are you with adapting your trading strategy based on changing market conditions?

A. Very comfortable (4 points)

B. Moderately comfortable (3 points)

C. Uncomfortable with adapting (2 points)

D. Resistant to change (1 point)

Example: Consider a shift in market conditions. If you adapt easily, 'A' is appropriate. If you resist changing your strategy even after many losses, 'D' may be more accurate.

10. Mindfulness in Trading:

How often do you practice mindfulness techniques to enhance focus and decision-making?

A. Regularly practice mindfulness (4 points)

B. Occasionally practice (3 points)

C. Rarely practice (2 points)

D. Do not practice mindfulness (1 point)

Example: Reflect on your mindfulness practices. If you incorporate mindfulness regularly, 'A' is fitting. If it's not part of your routine, 'C' or 'D' may be accurate.

Scoring and Interpretation:

40-32 points: Congratulations! You demonstrate a strong trading mindset.

31-24 points: You are on the right track but need to identify areas for improvement.

23-16 points: There's room for growth, focus on enhancing specific aspects of your mindset.

15-0 points: Consider areas where immediate changes can positively impact your trading psychology.

CHAPTER 3

THINKING IN PROBABILITIES

In this chapter, we are diving into the core stuff that will change your perspective about trading. Think of it as your main guide, the key to understanding how to handle the challenges of trading. We are talking about a big idea here – *thinking in probabilities*. Understanding that markets are unpredictable and every trade is like making an educated guess will help you make smart choices that last. This chapter is not just one part of the puzzle, it is the main piece.

Thinking in Probabilities: Why It Matters

There is one common mistake I observe new traders making. They patiently wait on the sidelines for the perfect moment and setups that practically tap them on the shoulder or shout at them to take notice. They are after trades that look picture-perfect, making it clear that it is the right time to jump into action.

It should not be your job to wait around for the ideal delivery to hit a six. Your job is to think in probabilities, to think in numbers and expectancy. This becomes easy to understand if you know how to play poker. I recommend searching on Google to understand the rules of poker before proceeding further. There is a rule in poker called *positive expectancy*. It is about playing without waiting for your power hands to show up. Given their favorable expectancy, you should play your medium-strength hands in a suitable setting.

Yes, you can hold out on joining the pot until AA or AK are suited, but in the long run, you will be losing out on a lot of profitable hands. Positive expectancy hands are the ones you are passing up.

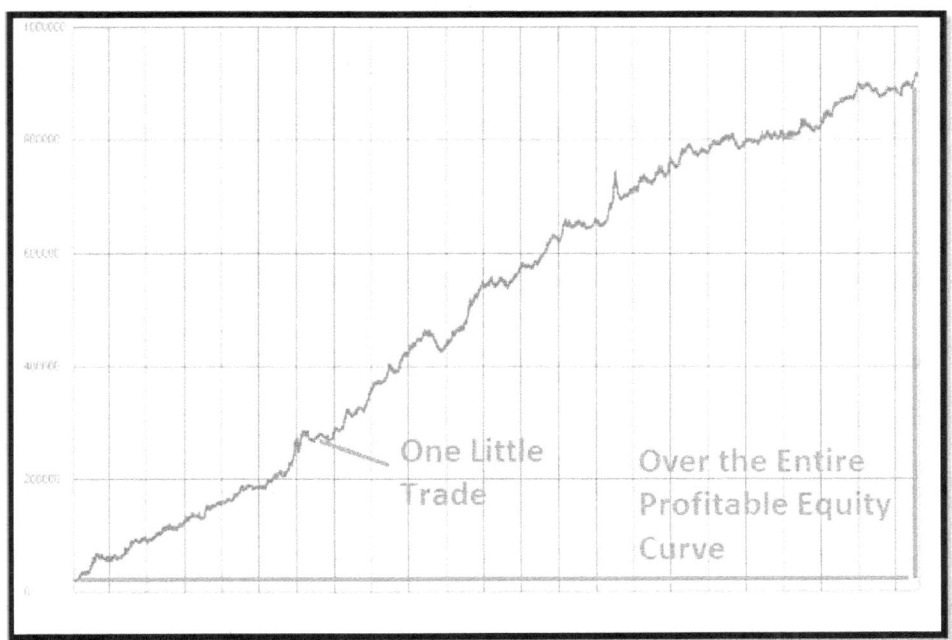

Similarly, the myth about waiting for perfect setups to trade is a misconception accepted by people who do not understand trading.

Traders use probability to think and identify setups that have a 100, 1,000, or 10,000x return on investment potential.

You must understand that even though the trade might not be profitable for you now, or in the future, you should continue to trade if there is a good chance (positive expectancy) of profit in the long run.

Successful traders do not worry about making or losing money on their next trade. Their primary focus is long-term and consistent income. By using technical analysis and adopting a probabilistic mindset, they aim to maximize their profits.

Though new traders base their entire mindset, confidence, and performance on the next trade, you must see the next trade as merely one of many free-throw attempts you will make in the future.

Mindset Shift: Embracing Probability over Certainty.

Traders must be prepared to change their way of thinking and accept that the market is not always predictable.

A significant component of this shift in perspective is accepting losses. It is normal to have trading losses, and it doesn't always indicate that you did something incorrectly.

Even with a well-thought-out trading plan, things may not your way as *anything can happen in the market.*

Observing this keeps traders resilient and prevents them from feeling like failures. This shift in perspective is realizing you will not always know everything when trading. Consider the likelihood of many outcomes rather than always wanting to be certain about something. Recognize that losses are common and they do not always indicate that your strategy is flawed. This adjustment makes your trading strategy stronger and more adaptable.

Understanding Random Outcomes:

Casinos make consistent profits daily, facilitating an event that has a purely random outcome. Most traders believe that the outcome of the market's behavior is not random, yet cannot seem to produce consistent results.

Here is the Key: Casinos, experienced gamblers, and the best traders have an understanding that the typical trader does not. Events that have probabilistic outcomes can produce consistent results if you can get the odds in your favor and there is a large enough sample size.

The best traders treat trading like a numbers game, similar to how casinos and professional gamblers approach gambling.

What casino owners and professional gamblers understand about the nature of probabilities is that each hand played is statistically independent of every other hand. This means that each hand is a "unique event," where the outcome is random, relative to the last hand played or the next hand played.

Think of a person at the roulette table deciding whether to bet on red or black. They know the spin of the wheel is a mix of luck and chance. Casinos always have a little advantage or edge because of the 2 green numbers added on the wheel.

Developing a new Belief that is contradictory to our thinking

▸ BLACKJACK	▸ TRADING
▸ Casino's "edge": 4.5%	▸ Trader's "edge": His methodology
▸ Rules: The House must play every hand…no exceptions	▸ Rules: Trader must execute every trade setup as defined by his methodology
▸ For each hand played there will be an unequal distribution of winning and losing hands.	▸ For each trade executed there will be an unequal distribution of winning and losing trades.
▸ On a collective basis, just the opposite is true…If enough hands are played, patterns will emerge that produce a consistent, predictable, statistically reliable outcome.	▸ On a collective basis, just the opposite is true. If the trader's methodology has a positive "edge", then many trades should produce consistent, predictable, statistically reliable outcome.

The Casino knows even if people are winning in the short term, they will be profitable in the long run as the odds are in their favor. Traders can use the same advantage of having an edge by using backtested and working trading strategies that tilt the odds of the trades in their favor, just like the casino.

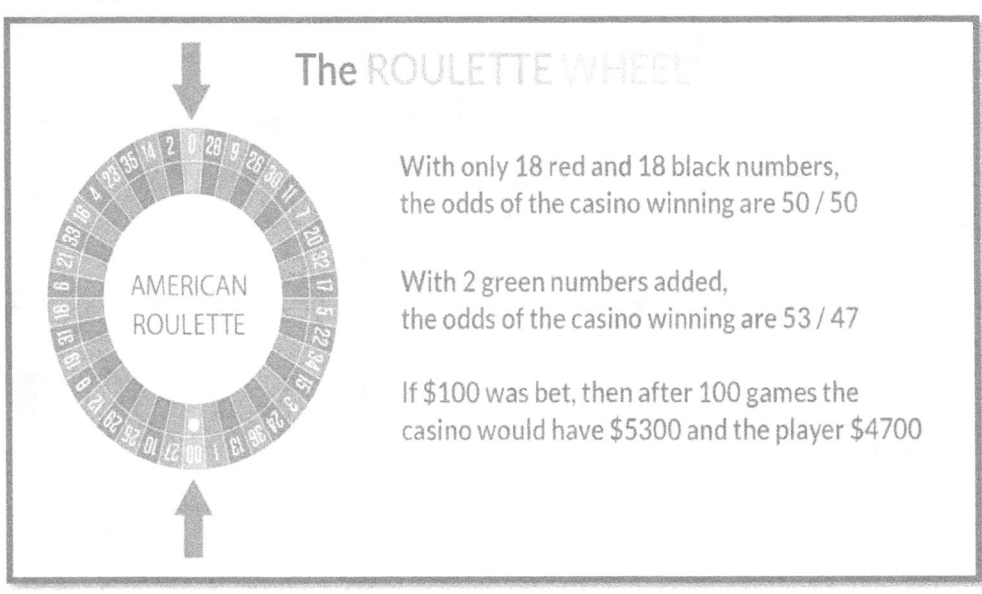

The ROULETTE WHEEL

AMERICAN ROULETTE

With only 18 red and 18 black numbers, the odds of the casino winning are 50 / 50

With 2 green numbers added, the odds of the casino winning are 53 / 47

If $100 was bet, then after 100 games the casino would have $5300 and the player $4700

Whether you're in a casino or trading, understanding that things can be unpredictable and accepting the randomness will surely get you closer to being a successful trader.

So, as you step into trading, think of yourself as a casino with an edge in the market (your trading strategy) to make sure you come out ahead in the long run.

When it comes to trading, individual results are like tossing a coin, you never know if a trade will turn out to be a profit or a loss. It is an unpredictable system affected by different market variables. But the real power is in the statistics, and the bigger the sample size you collect. Think about this: Making a single trade is similar to tossing a coin once, you can obtain heads for a profitable trade or tails for a losing one. It lacks clarity and makes it difficult to assess the strategy's success rate.

Now, consider tossing the coin 100 times but this time by putting some extra weight on the head side, this completely changes the probabilities, the coin will start landings on heads due to the extra added weight.

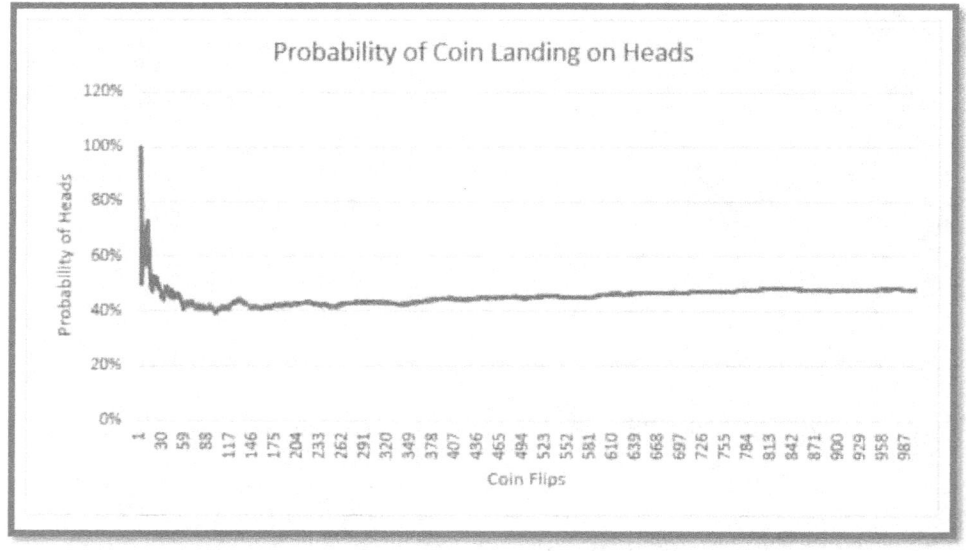

Putting weight on the head side of the coin is similar to having an edge or a trading strategy that will tilt the odds in your favor, and when you combine that with a big sample size, your strategy displays its win percentage together with other data, providing a statistical indicator of performance and confidence for you to execute the strategy without hesitation.

Importance of Sample Size in Trading:

Something is captivating about mathematics, it is clear-cut with no room for uncertainty. Mathematics is not a matter of opinion, 2+2 equals 4, and that's the final word, regardless of anyone's insistence otherwise. Numbers are truthful.

As someone with a commerce background, my affinity for numbers has greatly influenced my approach to trading from the very beginning. I never felt at ease relying on subjective predictions or following other traders' recommendations. I required solid, black-and-white evidence with real, concrete numbers to convince me that the trading rules and strategies I employed held a statistical advantage and were consistently profitable.

Every trading rule or strategy that I encountered, whether from books, courses, or fellow traders, I diligently tested to verify its profitability. Unsurprisingly, most strategies scrutinized over the past 14 years turned out to be misleading, some even originating from renowned and highly respected traders.

Out of nearly a hundred tested trading strategies, only a few consistently generated profits in the market. While assessing a strategy's past performance is relatively straightforward, the real challenge lies in predicting its future profitability.

Can we reasonably expect the strategy to yield the same results in the future as it did in the past? The likelihood is low since markets are ever-changing. To increase the likelihood of developing a trading strategy that not only proved effective in the past but also stands a good chance of success in the future, we must test the strategy in every market scenario.

Can we have confidence in numbers?

A widespread mistake by discretionary traders is to look only at small sample sizes (typically less than 100 trades) when building a strategy or deciding on a trading rule. Couple this with the human tendency to see what you want to see, relying on manually performed subjective strategy tests can quickly go wrong.

Performing tests manually often leads to errors and overconfidence in the test results. The only way to be confident in your statistics is if it is performed in an automated way with a testing algorithm applied to a large enough data set.

What size sample is large enough?

How to know if the results are due to pure luck or are statistically significant?

Don't worry, there is a formula for this.

It is called **Cochran's Sample Size Formula.**

$$\frac{Z^2 pq}{e^2}$$

- Z is Z score
- p is the currently known result (for example 50%-win rate for the strategy)
- q is 1-p
- e is the margin of error (for example 5%)

With this formula, we can calculate how many trades we need to have in our sample size to be confident in the statistical result, given our margin of error. This test is commonly used with a 5% margin of error.

Putting some figures into the formula we get:

Confidence level 99%

(2.58)^2 (0.5)(0.5)/0.05^2 = 666

To be 99% confident with a projection that has a 5% margin of error we need 666 trades in our sample.

Confidence level 95%

$(1.96)^2 (0.5)(0.5)/0.05^2 = 385$

To be 95% confident with a projection that has a 5% margin of error we need 385 trades in our sample.

Confidence level 90%

$(1.645)^2 (0.5)(0.5)/0.05^2 = 271$

To be 90% confident with a projection that has a 5% margin of error we need 271 trades in our sample.

Confidence level 80%

$(1.28)^2 (0.5)(0.5)/0.05^2 = 164$

To be 80% confident with a projection that has a 5% margin of error we need 164 trades in our sample.

Confidence level 70%

$(1.03)^2 (0.5)(0.5)/0.05^2 = 107$

To be 70% confident with a projection that has a 5% margin of error we need 107 trades in our sample.

To be 70% confident in your statistical result, you need at least 107 trades in your test sample, to be 99% confident you need 666 trades. A commonly accepted confidence level is 95%, thus when you have 385 trades in your test sample, you can be reasonably confident that the results are not obtained by chance.

Having a large enough sample size is very important when testing and developing trading strategies. If you are using small sample sizes you risk picking up random noise obtained by chance alone. That is not a good way to build your strategies. The larger the sample size the more confidence you can have in the statistical result.

Example:

Meet Priyanka and Digvijay, two traders trying out the same trading plan but with different amounts of practice. Priyanka is doing a lot, 300 trades, while Digvijay is doing a bit less, just 50 trades.

Imagine Priyanka in the first situation, doing 300 trades, she will have a big collection of information. This big group of trades helps Priyanka figure out if the plan works well in different market situations. She can see patterns and understand what the plan is good at and where it might need improvement.

Now, think about Digvijay in the second situation, doing only 50 trades. This small sample size makes it hard for Digvijay to make solid conclusions. The numbers might not be reliable, and it is tough to say how well the plan is doing.

When you have a small group of trades like Digvijay, there is a higher chance of making mistakes. If the plan is too focused on past data, it might not work well when things change in the market. This is called "overfitting." Priyanka, with the bigger group of trades, has less risk of this happening because the plan has faced a lot more situations.

Having more trades like Priyanka also gives more chances to learn, with each trade, there is something new to understand. So, in the end, having a bigger group of trades leads to more experiences to learn from. It helps us to adapt and improve the plan based on a wide range of situations in the market.

Practical Strategies to Improve Probabilistic Mindset:

Maintain a Trading Journal:

Keeping a trading journal is like creating a diary for your trades. It helps you develop a mindset that understands the uncertainties in trading. In this journal, write down the details of every trade, why you made the trade, and what happened in the end.

It is not just a record of your trades but also a tool to help you accept the unpredictable nature of the markets.

Reasons and Results:

Write down why you decided to make a trade. Include any technical or fundamental analysis you used to make your decision. Also, note if the trade ended up making you money or if you had a loss.

Regular Check:

Keep looking at your trading journal regularly. Try to see if there are patterns in the way you make decisions. See if what you thought would happen matches with what happened. This helps you learn and improve your strategy over time.

Big Picture:

To understand how trading works, make sure your journal covers a good number of trades over time. This bigger collection of recorded trades gives you a better idea of how well your strategy is working and helps you understand the probabilities involved.

Set Realistic Expectations:

Thinking in probabilities means being realistic about how successful you can be in trading. Here are some simple principles to keep in mind:

Not Just One Trade:

Know that whether a trade is a success or not does not tell the whole story. Look at how well your strategy works over many trades to see if it is consistent and reliable.

Look at Many Trades:

Check how good your strategy is by looking at its performance over many trades. This gives you a better overall picture of how well your trading system is doing and matches with the unpredictable nature of the market.

Think Long-Term:

When you are thinking about how successful you are in trading, try to think long-term. Understand that, over time, you will see how well your strategy is doing. This helps you change and improve your approach for success over the long run. Including these ideas in your trading can help you have a mindset that understands the uncertainties in the market. It also helps you adjust and make better decisions in the unpredictable world of trading.

In closing, remember a couple of key things. First, think in probabilities. Markets are unpredictable, so shift from wanting sure things to understanding that losses happen, and that's okay. Focus on how your strategy performs in the long run, not just one trade.

Second, understand the power of sample size. Small numbers of trades can be misleading. Larger numbers give a clearer picture. Be careful not to change your strategy too much based on just a few trades, randomness plays a role in the short term.

Practical tips matter. Keep a simple trading journal to learn from your experiences. Realize that one trade does not decide success or failure – it is the overall pattern.

As you keep going, keep thinking in probabilities and making informed choices.

CHAPTER 4

MANAGING EMOTIONS

Your worst enemy is yourself. When we say that, it sounds as mundane as it is unclear. But it is also very true. The three most important components of successful trading the markets are money management, strategy, and psychology. A professional trader must be able to handle all three. The truth is, even though you may have a winning strategy due to your built-in analytical nature and extensive training in technical analysis and market research, your ability to manage your emotions during trading will ultimately determine your level of success.

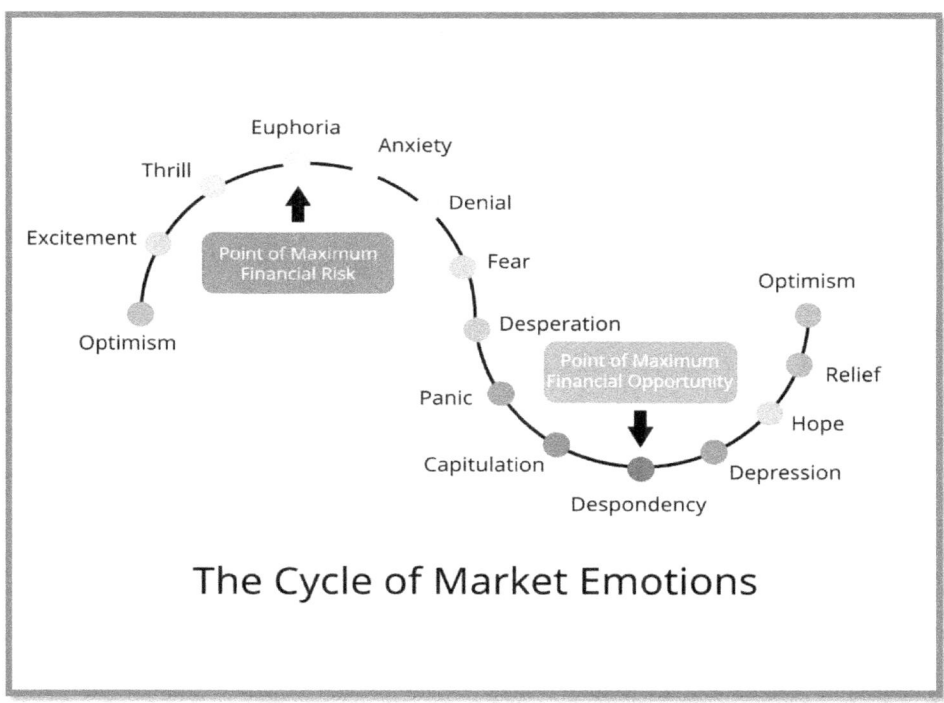

The Cycle of Market Emotions

In a survey conducted in 2021 by Jared Tendler on trading psychology around 1273 participants were studied out of which 89% were men and 11% were women, following statistics were revealed which gave a very insightful but disappointing look into traders' psychology and how emotions play a vital role in trading:

- 96% of traders acknowledge that emotions can negatively impact trading decisions.
- 91% can identify when emotions like fear, greed, and overconfidence affect their performance.
- Surprisingly, only 34% have a structured system to manage these emotions.

Emotions traders struggled the most with:

1. Fear (47%)
2. Lack of Confidence (22%)
3. Overconfidence (15%)
4. Greed (13%)

This data underscores the vital role emotions play in trading, echoing sentiments from seasoned professionals like Steve Burns. Despite high awareness, a substantial gap exists between recognition and implementation.

Notably, 57% of traders recognize emotional impacts but lack a strategy for management, prompting a call for change. This chapter aims to address this gap, offering actionable insights to empower traders in developing robust emotional management strategies for sustained success in the markets.

Common Emotional Challenges:

Fear and Loss Aversion:

When we trade, sometimes we get scared of losing money. This fear makes us do weird things, like selling a stock too early even if it is making money. Or, we might hesitate to jump into good opportunities we found. This fear messes with our profits and slows down the growth of our overall trading journey as we keep on missing chances and not making the best choices because we fear losing.

Greed and Overtrading:

When we want more money, it can lead to a common problem such as overtrading. This happens when we trade too much, take on too much risk, and start making decisions without thinking them through. Overtrading is like a trap that can cause unnecessary losses, make us tired, and even mess up how we make trading decisions.

Lack of Confidence in Trading:

Imagine feeling uncertain about your trading decisions, often underestimating your abilities. This is what we refer to as a lack of confidence in trading. It occurs when doubt clouds your judgment, leading to hesitation and missed opportunities. This lack of belief in your skills can impede your progress and hinder your overall success in the market.

Confirmation Bias:

Imagine having a favorite idea and only paying attention to things that agree with it. That is what we call confirmation bias, it is when we only accept information that supports what we already believe, and we might ignore anything that says otherwise. This bias can mess with how fair and open-minded we are. It might stop us from making smart decisions because we are not considering all the information. And sometimes, it means we miss chances to do better.

Detailed Strategies to Overcome Emotional Challenges:

Stay Mindful:

Incorporate simple yet effective mindfulness techniques into your trading routine. Before, during, and after your trading sessions, take moments for deep breathing exercises or brief meditation sessions. These practices not only enhance focus but also promote emotional balance, ensuring you approach your trades with a clear and calm mind. Headspace is one such app that provides quick guided meditations which will help you get into a calm mental state.

Write It Down

Create a comprehensive journal that includes the reasoning behind entering or exiting a trade, your emotional responses before the trade, throughout the trading process, and reflections after the trade concludes. This practice becomes your guide, facilitating a deeper understanding of your trading psychology and serving as a source for continuous enhancement.

Use platforms like Notion and Evernote to create your trading journals.

Here is an example of documenting your trades:

Start by recording the basic metrics:

Stock –

Order Type –

Entry Date –

Exit Date –

Timeframe -

Risk to Reward Ratio –

Strategy Name –

Take screenshots of your technical charts every time you enter and exit a stock.

Trade Screen Shots:

- Entry Chart

- Exit Chart

_____

(Record your emotions before, while, and after the trade.)

Emotions –

_____

(Answer the review questions to understand your trading mindset and mistakes)

Review Questions

After reviewing this trade one more time, has your analysis changed?

-

Did I follow my trading plan when analyzing, executing & managing this position?

-

Could I have entered or managed the trade better?

-

What happened after the trade was closed out?

-

Final Thoughts and lessons learned?

-

Have a Plan:

Trading is undeniably difficult. Nobody can ever predict with certainty how the markets will behave on any day. Profitable traders view trading as a lifetime pursuit in which there are always things to learn. This always includes making errors as well.

Trading is psychologically demanding. Your trading plan will be useful in all situations, but even more so during the difficult moments of your trading career. Your plan becomes crucial to the decisions you make when things do not seem to be going your way. Consider it your self-agreement, sticking to your plan will help you stay focused, and on the course, prevent hindsight bias, and achieve your long-term objectives.

Invest time in developing a well-defined trading plan that encompasses clear risk management rules, and precise entry, and exit.

Here are the steps to create your own Trading Business Plan:

A trading business plan is just like another business plan. It is a document that mentions everything you need to know to run your trading business.

Steps:

Have your mission statement for trading

E.g.: "To be the best trader I can be."

Write down your own goals and objectives for trading: You must spell out your trading/investing Goals and Objectives. You cannot get from A to B very easily unless you truly know where B is.

Write down your beliefs about trading by answering these simple questions:

1. What do I believe about the market?
2. What do I believe about trading?
3. What trading concepts do I believe work?
4. What risk management principles work?
5. How do the best traders trade?
6. What are the secrets to making money in the markets?

Now, after answering the questions put all these under beliefs examination tests:

1. Who gave me the belief—where did it come from?
2. What does this belief get me into? List at least five things.
3. What does this belief get me out of? List at least five things.
4. Is this belief useful, or is there a more useful belief?
5. Does this belief limit me?
6. How could I change it so that it is less limiting?
7. If I can't change it, is there a charge on the belief?
8. If it's appropriate, ask questions such as, "How do I define that?" and "How do I know?"

Your Trading Strategies:

1. What setups do you use before entry?

2. What is your timing signal for entry?

3. What is your worst-case loss going to be, and how is it determined?

4. How will you take profits?

5. What is the expectancy of that methodology? How good is the system?

6. How easy will it be with this system to use position sizing to achieve your goals?

Position Sizing

- What are your Position Sizing Strategies?

Dealing with Challenges:

1. What do I need to do daily to keep myself disciplined and on track?

2. What are the major emotional issues that come up for me, and how will I deal with them?

3. What is my ongoing plan for working on myself so that self-sabotage is avoided?

4. How can I make myself more efficient as a trader?

5. How can I recognize problems as they come into my trading and deal with them before they become self-sabotage?

Daily Procedures:

1. Do you need a pre-start-of-day self-assessment? What would that consist of? How will you do it?

2. How will you make sure that you do what you need to do today?

3. What will you do daily to prevent mistakes?

4. What will you do daily to keep track of your trades and your thoughts about trading?

5. What statistics will you monitor to keep track of your trading?

6. What will you do daily to work on yourself?

Educational Plan:

1. What do you need to know to improve your trading in terms of both skills and knowledge?

2. What do you need to improve about yourself to improve your performance?

3. How will you get that information?

Create a comprehensive trading business plan by answering all these questions.

Ask Questions:

Fear is an intense and destructive emotion that traders often encounter. When you are watching your trades unfold, keep asking yourself: *"Am I scared?"*

At any point, if you answer "Yes." Exit immediately.

Review your trading rules, reduce your trading size, and repeat.

Try asking yourself,

"Why am I selling?" to see if you are in command.

"Why won't I sell?"

"Why did I start this trade to begin with?"

"Why would or wouldn't I make this trade?"

If any of the responses are caused by impatience, fear, greed, or boredom, then you are not in charge. And because of those impulsive choices, you may suffer large losses. Our emotions are so powerful that it may take a while to realize who is in control until we start to act logically, by which point the damage has already been done

Do not check your P&L while in a trade:

I can hardly think of a figure that causes a greater surge of emotions than your profit and loss figure. For many traders, the profit and loss figure is an expression of their self-worth. (Nope. You are greater than just your profit and loss.) If you follow the most important trading rule and have a daily loss limit in place, you are already protected from severe losses.

Hence, you do not need to check your profit and loss figures constantly.

Talk to Others:

Actively participate in trading communities, and forums, or seek mentorship from experienced traders. Share your own experiences and challenges, and be open to receiving feedback. The exchange of ideas not only enhances your knowledge base but also fosters a collaborative learning environment, enriching your overall trading journey.

CHAPTER 5

BUILDING CONFIDENCE

Confidence in trading is not a mere state of mind, it is a dynamic force that shapes the trajectory of your trading journey. Your confidence influences the decisions you make, the strategies you deploy, and ultimately, your success in the market. A confident trader exhibits a greater ability to stick to their trading plan, make calculated decisions under uncertainty, and weather the storms of market volatility with resilience. This chapter dives into the important role of confidence and unveils practical steps to fortify this difficult attribute.

The Role of Confidence in Decision-Making:

Confidence plays a big role in trading decisions. When a trader feels confident, they are more likely to stick to their plans and strategies, even when the market is unpredictable. Confidence acts like a mental anchor, helping traders make decisions based on careful analysis instead of reacting emotionally. It gives traders the courage to be proactive, take advantage of opportunities, and handle risks calmly.

Interplay Between Confidence and Risk Management:

Confidence and good risk management go hand in hand in trading. When a trader feels sure about their decisions, they are better at setting and sticking to safe risk levels. A confident trader is more likely to set realistic limits on how much risk they take, making sure they stay balanced. This chapter talks about how having confidence helps traders make smart choices about managing risks, keeping their money safe, and boosting their chances of success in the long run.

Practical Steps to Boost Confidence:

Setting Achievable Goals

Realistic goals are the cornerstone of a fulfilling journey, they cultivate a sense of accomplishment. Break down those long-term goals into bite-sized, achievable milestones. It is like building a staircase, each step gets you closer to the top.

Example:

Rather than aiming for a huge profit in one go, set a goal for regular, smaller wins. This approach not only boosts your confidence but also ensures you're consistently moving forward, celebrating victories along the way. You can use the **SMART** Formula to set your trading goals.

Setting SMART goals is a straightforward and effective way to turn your aspirations into achievable objectives. SMART stands for Specific, Measurable, Achievable, Relevant, and Time-Bound.

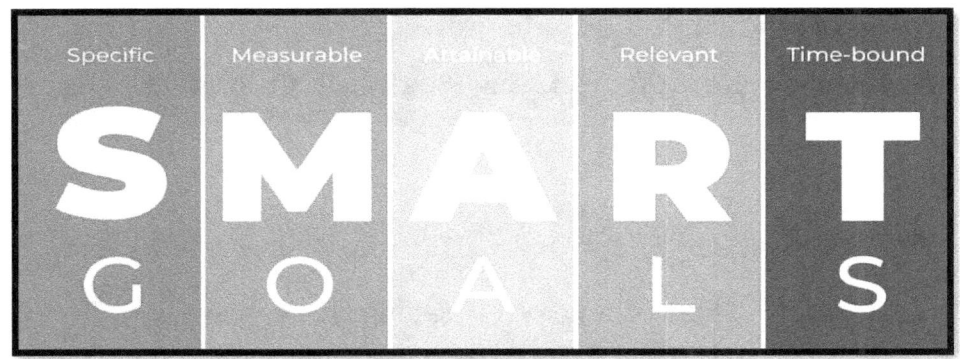

Here is a simple guide on how to set SMART goals:

Specific (S):

Goal: "I want to increase my monthly trading profits."

Specific Version: "I want to increase my monthly trading profits by 15% through more precise entry and exit points."

Measurable (M):

Goal: "I want to be a better trader."

Measurable Version: "I want to achieve a consistent 5% return on investment per month by the end of the quarter."

Achievable (A):

Goal: "I want to become a millionaire through trading within a year."

Achievable Version: "I want to grow my trading account by 35% over the next year, acknowledging the risks in the market."

Relevant (R):

Goal: "I want to learn about every trading strategy available."

Relevant Version: "I want to enhance my swing trading skills by studying and applying Price Action, as it aligns with my trading style."

Time-Bound (T):

Goal: "I want to be a full-time trader."

Time-Bound Version: "I want to transition to full-time trading within the next two years, starting by dedicating two hours daily to my trading education and practice."

Start a Demo Account

It is recommended to begin with a demo account if you're new to day trading. You can practice trading with a demo account without having to risk any real money. This is an excellent method for getting a sense of the ups and downs of day trading.

These are some websites where you can start demo trading:

1. Tradingview
2. Neostock
3. Moneybhai
4. Dalal Street

Start Small

It is crucial to start small when you are initially starting. Avoid attempting to trade with a large amount of capital as this will raise your risk of losing money. Additionally, it is critical to only trade with funds that you can afford to lose. You can start increasing your trade size when you've generated some steady profits with a small amount of money.

20 to 40k will be a good amount to start trading in the equity segment and as you build confidence and your trading capital, you can shift to trade futures and options.

Here are some strategies to grow a small trading account.

It is far harder to trade a small account than a huge amount. Small accounts lack the buffer that large accounts have against errors, unanticipated losing streaks, and occasionally even poor traders.

It is more difficult to trade well with a tiny account due to psychological reasons, even if you can afford losing streaks. For instance, a trader is under tremendous pressure to make a profitable deal when they are aware that they can only afford to lose one trade before their account is rendered untradeable due to insufficient margin.

Proper Risk Management:

To begin with, be sure you are entering each trade with the appropriate level of risk. This is less than 2% of the trader's whole account for the majority of them. Consider taking 1% or less at first if you're just getting started, and go up from there. Yes, it appears that you won't see a significant increase in your account balance by taking such a modest risk.

Here is the deal, though:

The key to growing a tiny trading account is perseverance. Over time, consistent victories add up to significant sums. Additionally, you won't have an account to trade with if you lose all of your money. Hence, the secret is to take a little risk while figuring out how to win far more often than you lose.

Don't Take Your Money Out:

It can be tempting to withdraw money to pay bills or purchase goods once you start making money from trading. But you should fight the urge to take money out of your account if you want to see rapid growth in it. Allow compounding to work its magic on your behalf. While you are building your account, look for additional ways to pay your payments.

Don't Compare yourself

Comparing oneself to others might be a simple task. Most of us are hardwired to do it from an early age. However, comparing oneself to others typically results in feelings of inadequacy, irritation, and frustration. In trading, your only real competition is yourself. Thus, cheer for successful traders. However, don't compare your achievement to what you believe you "should" be.

There isn't a "should."

Just the truth of where you are right now and the effort needed to get there. Put an end to your Instagram feeds for #lifeofatrader and #bitcoinbillionaire, and start working.

Look for ways to improve trading strategies:

Okay, let's move on to the topic of trading strategies. Struggling traders often switch between systems in an attempt to make enormous profits. In reality, though, you might be able to just "turn up the volume" on your regularly successful approach.

To improve your trading strategy, set clear financial goals and understand your risk tolerance. Utilize effective risk management, diversify your investments, and stay informed about market trends. Backtest your strategy for insights, be adaptable to changing market conditions, and leverage technology for efficiency. Maintain emotional discipline, review and learn from your trades regularly, and engage with other traders for insights. Lastly, evaluate your broker and platform to ensure they meet your needs. This comprehensive approach, focusing on goal-setting, risk management, adaptability, continuous learning, and technology, can enhance the effectiveness of your trading strategy.

Focus on the trading process:

Your trading strategy is not nearly as critical as your process and mindset. Conduct beta and backtesting before making any trades on your live account. This procedure is crucial as it provides you with valuable information on a trading strategy and its effectiveness.

It also enables you to concentrate on particular aspects of your trading to determine whether they function well on their own. It's simpler to identify the problems when you split them down in this way.

It is quite difficult to determine whether your problems are with risk management, strategy, or mindset if you immediately start live trading.

Review your spending:

While creating a trading account, you might not have considered looking in this area, but it offers the potential for a simple win. Start by keeping track of your spending for a month. Make use of a journal, spreadsheet, or app. whichever suits your needs. Make sure you keep a record of everything you purchase. Examine your monthly expenses at the end of the month. Is there a way you can cut back on your spending? It's possible that you can or cannot.

I'm not advocating living a monastic lifestyle without a morning cup of coffee. However, perhaps you don't have to visit Starbucks each week.

Create cashflows for your trading capital:

Lastly, look for methods to enhance your life with additional low-maintenance cashflow sources. Lots of money is sitting around in

most parts of the world. Not money exactly, but rather chances to earn money. The ability to recognize these resources and transform them into reliable sources of revenue is the skill. Invest all of the money you make from this new venture into your expanding trading account. You can considerably increase the amount in your trading account with just one extra source of income. Thus, have an open mind about novel techniques to generate income.

6 Easy Visualization Techniques

To Use RIGHT Now!

1.) Meditation

2.) Guided Hypnosis

3.) Vision Boards

4.) Playing it out in everyday life

5.) Law of Attraction groups or forums

6.) Manifestation journal

Visualization Techniques:

Visualization is not just a mental exercise, it is a powerful tool that boosts mental preparedness and confidence. Before making trades, take a moment to picture successful outcomes in your mind.

Example:

Close your eyes and imagine yourself calmly navigating through market fluctuations, following your trading plan, and achieving positive outcomes. This mental rehearsal through visualization not only prepares you for success but also instills the confidence needed to execute your trades with precision and poise.

Here is the Visualization Technique I use every day before trading –

- Find a quiet and comfortable space to sit, close your eyes, and take a few deep breaths to center yourself. Sync your breath with a mental count: Inhale for a count of four, hold for four, and exhale for four. Repeat.
- Visualize the entire trading process from analysis to execution.
- Imagine successful outcomes, following your trading plan, executing trades perfectly, managing risks, and adapting to market changes.

Positive Self-Talk:

Positive affirmations aren't just words, they're the building blocks of a confident mindset. Whenever negative thoughts creep in, replace them with affirmations highlighting your trading abilities. It's a powerful way to reshape your mental landscape.

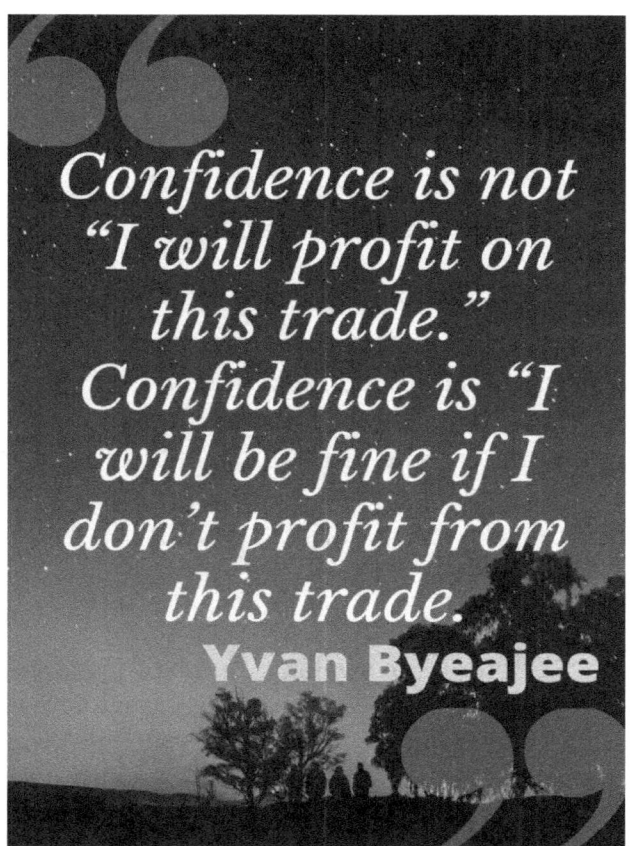

Confidence is not "I will profit on this trade." Confidence is "I will be fine if I don't profit from this trade.
Yvan Byeajee

Example:

Rather than fearing losses, affirm your capability to manage risks effectively. During challenging times, remind yourself of past successful trades. These affirmations act as a shield against self-doubt, reinforcing your belief in your trading prowess.

- Set aside a few minutes each morning for trading affirmations.
- Craft positive and empowering affirmations related to your trading goals. ("I am a successful trader who manages risk well.")

- Repeat these affirmations aloud or in your mind, focusing on the positive impact they have on your mindset.

Here are 10 self-affirmations for traders.

1. I am confident in my trading abilities.

2. I have faith that my decisions are the right ones.

3. I trust my judgment and am not afraid to take risks.

4. I embrace change and understand that it is part of the trading process.

5. I focus on the long-term goals of my trading strategy.

6. I am patient and remain disciplined in my trading decisions.

7. I am determined to succeed in trading.

8. I accept that I will make mistakes and use them as learning experiences.

9. I stay committed to my trading goals.

10. I stay up-to-date with market trends and news.

Continuous Learning and Adaptation:

The more you learn, the more confident you become in navigating the complexities of different market conditions. Stay actively engaged in learning keep yourself informed about market trends, explore new strategies, and embrace adaptability as a key principle.

Example:

Attend webinars, delve into market analysis, and incorporate fresh insights into your trading approach. Establish a routine of learning from both successful trades and challenges. This commitment to continuous learning not only expands your knowledge base but also bolsters your confidence in making informed decisions.

Building confidence is not an overnight endeavor, it is a nuanced and gradual process. Regularly reflect on your progress, celebrate achievements, and remain adaptable. Confidence is not just a trait, it is a skill honed through continuous learning and practical application. As you embark on implementing these detailed and practical steps, remember that each stride toward confidence contributes to your growth as a resilient and successful trader.

CHAPTER 6

LIMITING BELIEFS

There was a set of twin brothers, Digvijay being the younger and Harsh the elder. They both attended the same school and even received their degrees from the same university. Despite their tendency towards individuality, both were exceptionally intelligent students. Harsh, being the oldest one, was more cautious and took fewer risks.

Digvijay, meanwhile, was more daring and willing to take chances. The brothers joined a trading course two years ago, and they had a great time. But after two years, Harsh is still having trouble turning a profit, whereas Digvijay continues to generate steady profits each month. Harsh is dissatisfied and feels that he is not meant to be rich even though he does not suffer significant losses.

As you can see, despite sharing a very similar upbringing and lifelong education, these brothers can achieve extremely distinct trading outcomes. To be honest, I just chose twin brothers to reinforce my point of view. Is there a trader you can think of who began their trading career later than you but is now significantly more skilled than you? Do you know of any trader who is performing significantly worse than you despite having traded for a longer period?

Moreover, *do you know why?*

Although there may be several factors separating Digvijay and Harsh, we can be positive that one of Harsh's shortcomings can be traced back to his limiting beliefs.

You see, it's important to have a strong and sound belief system, and it appears that Harsh has had one since he was a small child. His academic accomplishments would have given him more self-assurance and equipped him to overcome many challenges in the future.

While it is true that having a strong belief system is essential for success, it is equally true that having limiting beliefs can keep you from achieving your goals. One of Harsh's biggest limiting beliefs is that he does not think he will be rich. It might even have been the only thing keeping him from becoming profitable. This is because, even though adopting appropriate actions is a result of having a sound belief system, restricting beliefs will prevent you from acting on your desires. *Can you see the problem?*

Understanding Limiting Beliefs:

Limiting beliefs about trading might be a common response to the complexity of possible trading situations. As traders, we can occasionally tell our subconscious to believe that we will win most, if not all, of our trades. When we have built our systems in a way that we believe is unbreakable, it can be difficult to challenge those ideas. Then, we may hold these beliefs heavily accountable when we fail to meet our objectives or lose trade.

Limiting beliefs can be held to by some traders for a very long time. In numerous situations, traders must overcome any mental obstacles and limitations they may have placed on themselves. When a trader encounters any depressing or unpleasant feelings when trading, it may lead to the development of poor mental habits that prevent them from moving forward.

Regardless of whether you win or lose, you should strive to maintain balance to advance and achieve better trading outcomes. Typical limiting beliefs in trading include the following:

- **To make a profit, I have to work long hours and trade hard.**
- **I could never succeed if I put in too much work.**
- **To get decent returns, I must invest a lot of money.**
- **In trading, very few people come out on top.**
- **Living off the market is extremely difficult.**

As traders, our trading beliefs can shape our trading experience and ultimately dictate the course we take. We must separate ourselves from these beliefs to trade well, and we must keep our psychological balance under check. There are a lot of unfavorable attitudes and beliefs about the stock market after searching through various parts of the Internet for knowledge regarding trading. Many continue to wonder if it's possible to beat the market at all, who makes money in trading, and how to avoid losing money when using an account. Many traders who read these articles may believe this to be true, leading them to develop their own trading-related limiting beliefs.

A lot of trading is based on one's confidence and ability to predict whether a trade will be profitable or not.

Identifying Limiting Beliefs:

When trying to identify your limiting beliefs, you may find this simple formula helpful.

1st Step

Note down any goals that you are finding difficult to fulfill. For instance: I wish to become a successful trader.

2nd Step

Put down the reason(s) why you are unable to accomplish it. Example: I don't believe I'm capable of it.

3rd Step

Destroy those reasons:

- Confirming the untruth of those restricting ideas.
- Identifying previous instances in your life where you overcame doubts to accomplish goals.

Example: I'm not incapable of doing something just because I haven't done it before.

Alternatively, I've accomplished X and Y objectives in the past despite my belief that I would undoubtedly fail before doing so.

Methods to overcome Limiting Beliefs:

A few of our limiting beliefs are a result of past mistakes or disappointments. The mainstream media and even social media serve as fuel for other views. Others come from unfavorable connections with family, friends, coworkers, and religious communities. You don't have to let your views limit you, regardless of where they originated from or what they are. They can be replaced with empowering truths.

To assist you with that, here are six steps.

Recognize the Belief: A belief may be restricting if it is suggestive of a single way of thinking. Perhaps it comes from a relationship or previous work experience. It's important to understand that any view, no matter how strong or how accurate it seems, is merely an opinion about reality, and it's probably incorrect.

Record the Belief: This belief could be one of the following: "I'm not very disciplined," "I don't have enough experience in trading," or "I'm not good at trading." Since every one of us faces unique difficulties, it may be anything. Try writing down the belief exactly as it is spoken. You express it when you put it in writing. After that, you are free to assess it.

Review the belief. Does this belief help you reach your goals or does it get in the way of your success? Does it feel empowered or tiresome?

Make an effort to view things unbiased. Additionally, be truthful. The secret to freedom is an honest assessment.

Reject the belief: You can reject a limiting belief if it is untrue. From "I don't have the energy to walk 10,000 steps a day" to "I have the energy to walk 10,000 steps every day," there are instances where the transition is simple. More is needed to reframe a belief. Because there is usually some truth underlying limiting beliefs. It's not necessary to give in to a limiting belief, even if it holds some truth. The story can be revised. You may believe that you lack creativity. You may just give up and wait it out. Alternatively, you may phrase it like this: "I can always work with someone creative, even though I'm not creative."

Revise the belief: This goes beyond straightforward affirmations. It involves refocusing your thoughts on a fresh, free reality. You might believe, for instance, that you lack the precise experience required for that position. Saying "I have different experiences that will make me a more unique candidate" is a better alternative. You are held back by your outdated mindset, but you now have a foundation for genuine advancement. Make sure you also record the updated belief in writing.

Reorient yourself to the new belief: Start telling your story from this new, free truth. You may not agree with it entirely. You can even feel as though you are acting. That is acceptable. However, you will eventually get more at ease with the reality if you continue to tell yourself the truth.

CHAPTER 7

SETTING GOALS

The amount of money that you take from the market is outside your control. The number of setups you receive each week or month is beyond your control. How many of your transactions succeed in reaching your target price (TP) and how many fail is beyond your control. Of course, you can have reasonably precise statistics regarding your expectations and performance in the long run, but there are distinct guidelines in the short term. From week to week, anything can occur.

Thus, a trader's performance may suffer if their goals are results-based. Will you miss out on potentially profitable trades for the remainder of the week or month if you reach your objective early? If not, why did you set out with this objective in the first place?

You are more inclined to overtrade or take on excessive risk if you fall short of your objective. This will very certainly cause you to stray from your objective and result in poor trading performance overall.

And lastly, where do those results-based objectives originate from initially? What did you think about them? They're probably simply made up.

I have witnessed innumerable traders execute wishful-thinking computations in which they open a spreadsheet and calculate the required return in reverse to reach a fictitious target, such as making 1 crore in a specific amount of time. Your only job as a trader is to make the best trades possible, but you cannot control when they happen.

Every effective strategy or plan starts with an objective. We cannot declare a plan of action to be successful unless that objective is accomplished. This idea also holds for trading.

As you navigate the stock market, having realistic trading goals gives you direction and guidance. Setting goals helps you prioritize your tasks and make well-informed decisions by giving you something to strive for. They also assist you in staying on track so that you are not easily influenced by impulsive or emotional trading decisions.

Trading may be difficult and frustrating, particularly when there is a lot of market volatility. Setting goals forces you to remember why you are trading all the time, which increases drive and discipline. Setting clear objectives also gives you a helpful benchmark to gauge how well your present approach is working and how far you have come in trading. In this manner, you may make data-driven choices and gradually modify and improve your trading approach.

For example, if you are not reaching your objectives, you might assess your most recent trades to pinpoint areas that need work and implement corrective actions. However, if you are outperforming your targets, you may identify what is effective and build on it to increase your trading success.

The **Right** Trading Goals

Trading Goals Worth Adopting:

1. Fewer Mistakes:

Naturally, a trader who aims to make the fewest mistakes possible in each week or month would do better. Reduce the number of trades you chase, avoid entering too soon, stick to your principles, and be patient with the setups that gradually materialize in front of you to improve your entries. Additionally, search for better exits. Reducing any emotionally driven decisions, letting winners run longer, and properly cutting losses are ways to improve exits. Lastly, attempt to steer clear of any mistakes related to risk management, such as excessive trading, taking on excessive risk, or emotionally adjusting trades. An objective like that will undoubtedly improve your trading.

Practical Steps:

You can use the *Trading Discipline Quest*, which I and many of my students use to fastrack their trading by avoiding silly mistakes.

Challenge Duration:

The Trading Discipline Quest spans four weeks, providing sufficient time to establish and reinforce disciplined trading habits.

Component 1: Pre and Post-Trading Rituals

Pre-Trading Rituals:

- Develop a routine before starting your trading day.
- Include activities like reviewing market news, checking economic calendars, and setting specific goals for the day.
- Engage in a brief mindfulness exercise to focus your mind.

Post-Trading Rituals:

- Establish a routine for after your trading session.
- Reflect on the day's trades, noting successes and areas for improvement.
- Perform a quick analysis of your emotional state and assess adherence to your trading plan.

Here are Pre and Post Trading questions to ask yourself.

Pre-Trading Questions Examples:

1. What is my trading objective for this specific trade?
2. Have I thoroughly researched and analyzed the market conditions?
3. What is the risk-reward ratio for this trade?
4. Is my position size in line with my risk tolerance and overall strategy?

5. Have I set clear stop-loss and take-profit levels?

6. What potential risks and adverse scenarios should I be aware of?

7. Does this trade align with my overall trading plan?

Post-Trading Questions:

1. Did the trade unfold as planned?

2. Was the risk-reward ratio effective in this particular trade?

3. Did I adhere to my predetermined trading plan?

4. What lessons can I learn from the outcomes of this trade?

5. How have market conditions evolved since the trade was initiated?

6. Did I stick to the predetermined stop-loss and take-profit levels?

7. What adjustments, if any, should be made to my overall trading strategy?

8. How does this trade impact my portfolio balance and risk exposure?

Component 2: Print and Read Your Trading Plan

- Print a physical copy of your trading plan.
- Read through your trading plan before each trading session to reinforce your strategy and goals.

- Ensure that your trading decisions align with the principles outlined in your plan.

Component 3: Emotional Checklist Before Trading

- Create an emotional checklist to assess your mental state before trading.
- Include items such as stress levels, clarity of mind, and ability to handle potential losses.
- Use the checklist to gauge whether you are emotionally prepared for trading.

Use this rating template to track your emotions in trading:

Rate each question in this trading template to assess your emotions

Pre-Trading Emotional State:

Confidence Rating (1-10): _____

Tip: To boost confidence, conduct a thorough market analysis and focus on your prepared strategy. Confidence often comes from being well-prepared.

External Factors Impact (1-10): _____

Tip: Control external factors by creating a designated trading space. Minimize distractions and create an environment conducive to focused decision-making.

During Trades:

Stress Management (1-10): _____

Tip: Employ stress management techniques such as meditation or a quick walk. Develop a pre-trade routine to calm your mind before making decisions.

Discipline Adherence (1-10): _____

Tip: Enhance discipline by setting up predefined alerts for trade entries and exits. This helps automate your strategy and reduces the likelihood of impulsive decisions.

Patience Level (1-10): _____

Tip: Improve patience by practicing mindfulness. Consider incorporating short mindfulness exercises during trades to maintain focus on the present moment.

Fear/Excitement Management (1-10): _____

Tip: Manage fear and excitement by using a trading journal. Documenting emotions during trades helps identify patterns and develop strategies for emotional control.

Post-Trading Emotional State:

Satisfaction with Performance (1-10): _____

Tip: Analyze both wins and losses to derive meaningful insights. Celebrate successes and view setbacks as opportunities for growth.

Reflection on Wins/Losses (1-10): _____

Tip: Conduct a weekly review of your trades to identify recurring patterns. This reflection aids in refining your strategy and making more informed decisions.

Emotional Disconnect (1-10): _____

Tip: Create a post-trading routine to signal the end of your workday. Engage in a hobby or activity that helps shift your focus away from the market.

Handling Mistakes:

Reaction to Unplanned Trades (1-10): _____

Tip: Develop a checklist for analyzing trade outcomes. This systematic approach helps turn mistakes into valuable learning experiences.

Learning from Mistakes (1-10): _____

Tip: Foster a growth mindset by actively seeking feedback. Regularly review your trading decisions and seek input from mentors or peers to accelerate learning.

Overall Emotional Resilience:

Handling Ups and Downs (1-10): _____

Tip: Cultivate emotional resilience by visualizing your long-term goals. Remind yourself that short-term fluctuations are part of the journey toward success.

Emotions Impact on Decisions (1-10): _____

Tip: Use a decision-making checklist to ensure objectivity. This tool helps mitigate the influence of emotions on your trading decisions.

Maintaining Positive Mindset (1-10): _____

Tip: Develop a gratitude practice related to your trading journey. Regularly express gratitude for the lessons learned and progress achieved.

Discipline and Self-Control:

Adherence to Risk Management (1-10): _____

Tip: Implement a reward system for disciplined risk management. Celebrate milestones like consistent risk adherence to reinforce positive behavior.

Controlling Impulsivity (1-10): _____

Tip: Introduce a pause before executing trades. Take a moment to review your trading plan, ensuring decisions are deliberate rather than impulsive.

Reflection on Goals:

Alignment with Trading Goals (1-10): _____

Tip: Regularly revisit and update your trading goals. Ensure that your emotional reactions align with the broader objectives you've set for yourself.

Motivation for Improvement (1-10): _____

Tip: Keep a vision board featuring your trading goals. This visual reminder can boost motivation and serve as a constant source of inspiration.

Learning and Adaptation:

Openness to Learning (1-10): _____

Tip: Foster a learning mindset by participating in trading communities. Engage in discussions, share experiences, and seek insights from fellow traders.

Emotional Adaptation to Market Changes (1-10): _____

Tip: Develop contingency plans for different market scenarios. This preparation enhances emotional adaptation, ensuring you're ready for changing conditions.

Rate Your Day Emotionally: _____

Sign

Use this emotional tracker every day to keep your emotions in check.

Component 4: Daily Journaling of Trades

- Maintain a daily trading journal.
- Record details of each trade, including entry and exit points, reasons for the trade, emotional state, and any deviations from your plan.
- Use the journal as a tool for self-reflection and continuous improvement.

Component 5: Weekly Review of All Your Trades and Refining

- Conduct a comprehensive weekly review of all your trades.
- Analyze the overall performance, identifying patterns, strengths, and weaknesses.
- Refine your trading plan based on insights gained during the review.
- Set specific goals for improvement in the coming week.

Answer these reflection questions every week -

1. How was my mindset throughout the week?

2. Were there any distractions for my trading, if there were, did it influence my trading?

3. Did I follow my plan during the week?

4. Were there any trading mistakes during the week?

5. Am I aligned with my trading goals?

6. What should I improve or focus on going into the next week?

Reflection and Rewards:

Reflect on the impact of these disciplined practices on your trading performance. Consider implementing rewards for consistently adhering to your rituals and maintaining discipline throughout the challenge.

Maintaining discipline in trading is not just about sticking to a set of rules, it is about creating a sustainable and positive trading routine. The Discipline-Reward System is a powerful tool designed to reinforce positive behaviors and decisions.

Here is a practical framework for creating a discipline-reward system for yourself:

Identify Achievements:

- Break down your trading goals into specific, achievable milestones.
- Recognize both short-term accomplishments and long-term objectives.

Define Rewards:

- Select rewards that resonate with you whether it is a short break, a small treat, or a leisure activity.
- Ensure that the size of the reward corresponds to the significance of the achievement.

Establish Criteria:

Clearly outline the criteria for earning a reward. This could include faithfully following your trading plan, adhering to risk management principles, or achieving specific profit targets.

Consistency is Key:

- Consistency is crucial for the effectiveness of the Discipline-Reward System.
- Regularly review and, if necessary, adjust your goals and rewards to keep them aligned with your evolving trading journey.

2. Better Routine:

A more professional approach to trading might be established by many traders with ease by making simple improvements to their practice. Trading is a business, thus you must organize your trades accordingly. It can be a fantastic goal to journal all trades before the end of the day.

Journaling and establishing a genuine review practice are the best and most efficient ways to improve your trading. Investing half an hour each morning to review the previous day's events and update your charts will also help you stay consistent, get more organized, and miss fewer trades.

Practical Step:

Daily Trading Routine

A well-structured daily routine is your compass, guiding you through your trading journey. It ensures you stay aligned with your Trading Plan, providing a roadmap for success. Remember, adaptability is key – your routine should be flexible enough to accommodate your personality and life circumstances.

Below is an example of how you can create a trading routine for yourself.

1. Morning Routine:

- Wake-up Time and Pre-Trading Tasks:
- Attend to personal needs: bathroom, coffee, breakfast, etc.

- Glance over your daily plan for a quick reminder of tasks and priorities.

2. Mental Preparation:

- Clear your mind and assess your mental state.
- Identify and diminish inner conflicts, anxiety, or over-confidence.
- Strive for a neutral state before trading.
- Avoid trading when emotions are heightened, it rarely ends well.

3. Goal Reinforcement:

- Focus on your planned actions, not just the monetary outcomes.
- Remember, money results from consistent, well-executed actions.

4. Visualization and Trading Plan:

- Go through your Trading Plan to reinforce strategies.
- Mentally picture executing trades perfectly.
- Visualize both wins and losses; accept both as part of the journey.

5. Market Preparation:

- Compile a watchlist for the day and refine it based on recent developments.
- Stay informed about major news or earnings events that could impact trades.

6. Trading Time:

- Define a time frame for active trading.
- Allocate time for a break if needed – check emails, hydrate, grab a snack.
- Finish Trading
- Stick to your trading time limit.

7. Post-Trading Review:

- Review Daily/Weekly Trades:
- Take screenshots of trades for analysis.
- Identify mistakes and strengths.
- Develop an action plan for improvement.

8. Additional Tasks:

- Allocate time for workouts, activities, and personal tasks.
- Meditation on Trading Goals.

- Reflect on the type of trader you aspire to be and the steps to reach that goal.

Remember, consistency is key. Regularly update and refine your routine to ensure it remains effective and aligned with your evolving needs.

3. Self-Improvement:

The trader is typically the weakest link in any trading operation. Thus, you must work on yourself. Setting aside 30 minutes each day to read a book that is motivational, educational, or inspiring can lead to a wealth of fresh ideas. I'm sure someone far wiser than me has said it before, but in my experience, all it takes is a single, tiny new idea to start a massive fire that has the power to alter your entire life. Anyone who wants to enhance their quality of life should be required to meditate for a few minutes each morning or participate in any self-awareness program. But it's not enough to only train our minds. Daily exercise is a must to blow off steam and counteract all the negative effects that come from our sedentary lifestyle.

Practical Steps:

Reading Habits:

Cultivate a habit of reading not only about trading strategies but also literature from diverse genres. Fiction, non-fiction, and even autobiographies can offer valuable insights and broaden your understanding of various perspectives. Reading widely contributes to a well-rounded and adaptable mindset.

Exercise Routine:

Incorporate regular exercise into your daily routine. Physical activity has been shown to have positive effects on cognitive function and emotional well-being. Whether it's a morning run, gym session, or yoga practice, exercise can enhance your overall energy levels and mental resilience, crucial for navigating the challenges of trading.

Continuous Learning:

Identify areas outside of trading that can enhance your overall skills. Consider aspects like communication skills, time management, or even understanding macroeconomic trends. Enroll in relevant courses or workshops to systematically build proficiency in these areas.

Networking:

Expand your horizons by networking beyond the trading community. Attend industry events, join online forums, and connect with professionals from diverse fields. Insights from individuals outside the trading realm can provide fresh perspectives, influencing your mindset and decision-making.

Have a brain-boosting diet :

Incorporating brain-boosting foods into your diet can contribute to improved focus and cognitive function, essential for effective trading. Here are some examples of fruits known for their positive impact on brain health:

Blueberries: Packed with antioxidants, blueberries have been linked to improved memory and cognitive performance. The anthocyanins in blueberries may enhance brain function, making them an excellent choice for maintaining focus during trading sessions.

Bananas: A good source of energy, bananas provide a quick and easily digestible carbohydrate boost. They also contain vitamin B6, which plays a role in neurotransmitter production, aiding in concentration and focus.

Oranges: High in vitamin C, oranges contribute to overall immune system health. The antioxidant properties of vitamin C may also protect the brain from oxidative stress. Additionally, the natural sugars in oranges offer a quick energy boost.

Strawberries: Like blueberries, strawberries are rich in antioxidants and vitamin C. They may help reduce oxidative stress and inflammation in the brain, supporting cognitive function.

Walnuts: While not a traditional fruit, walnuts are rich in omega-3 fatty acids, which are essential for brain health. They may support cognitive function and help maintain focus.

CHAPTER 8

HANDLING LOSSES

Losses are a given in trading. Whenever one takes a stop loss, sadness is a common emotion. You feel better if the stock falls much farther after you exit. You feel dejected if the stock rises and reaches your target after hitting your stop loss. Do you recognize this? That is how Mr. Market wants you to respond.

Refrain from falling for it. Losses occur during trading. A new way of thinking needs to be acquired to lessen the stress and psychological suffering that come with losing.

Trading is a business, and like any business, trading requires deducting expenses from revenues to turn a profit. Losses should be viewed as a business expense. Without expenses, a firm cannot be run. Of course, you want to reduce those costs as much as possible to increase profits, but costs are an unavoidable part of running a firm. The most successful traders gain knowledge from their losses and apply that knowledge to become "wiser" the next time something similar happens. This is how defeats turn into chances to grow as a trader and advance your skill set.

Good Losses vs Bad Losses

Every loss is not created equal. Both positive and negative losses might occur. This distinction is based on the circumstances surrounding the loss rather than the amount that was lost.

Good losses: Good losses are the ones you take as planned and expected. It means you knew there could be both success and failure in the trade, and when things didn't go as planned, you sensibly followed your strategy by accepting the pre-determined stop-loss. The fact that you were prepared for it and took action makes it a positive loss.

Bad Losses: Bad losses are the result of deviating from your trading plan or not having one at all due to fear, stress, and/or panic. This can happen when you impulsively trade out of FOMO, or fear of missing out, entering a trade without a plan, enduring early setbacks until the pain becomes intolerable, and then quitting in a state of panic. Everyone experiences it at some point. Everybody faces unfortunate losses. Acknowledging and learning from them is crucial. Since they are the most agonizing kinds of losses, bad losses can teach you some of the most important lessons.

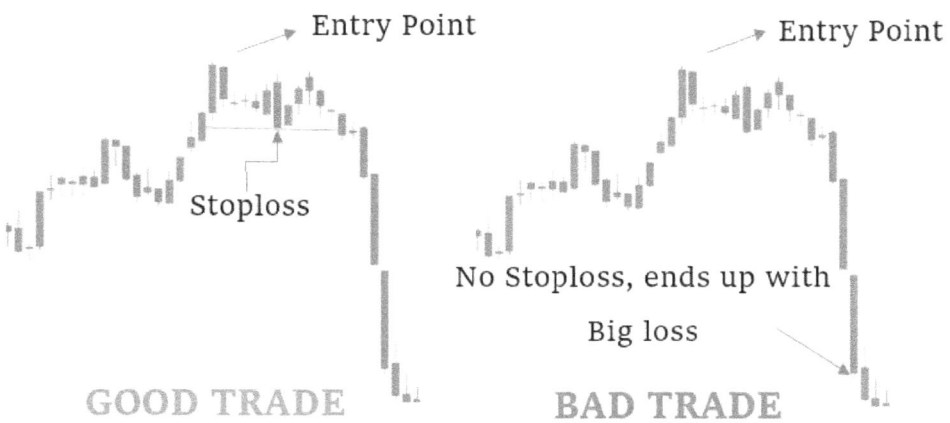

Strategies for Managing Losses:

1. Learn from losses:

The best fund managers and traders have discovered the hard way to make mistakes and how to learn from them to proceed correctly going forward. It is possible to use painful losses as a lesson on what not to do again. You soon learn not to touch a hot stove again after touching one.

Bad losses are those resulting from trading without a plan at all or from straying from it out of fear, worry, and/or panic. Everyone experiences it occasionally. Everyone has unfortunate losses. Recognizing and taking lessons from them is the key. Since severe losses are the most painful kind, they can teach you some of the most important lessons.

2. Diagnose the Loss:

This is where you get clinical. Review the trade as if you were a researcher in a lab. Diagnose where you should have taken the stoploss and what caused you to stray from the plan.

Below is a clear framework to diagnose your losses.

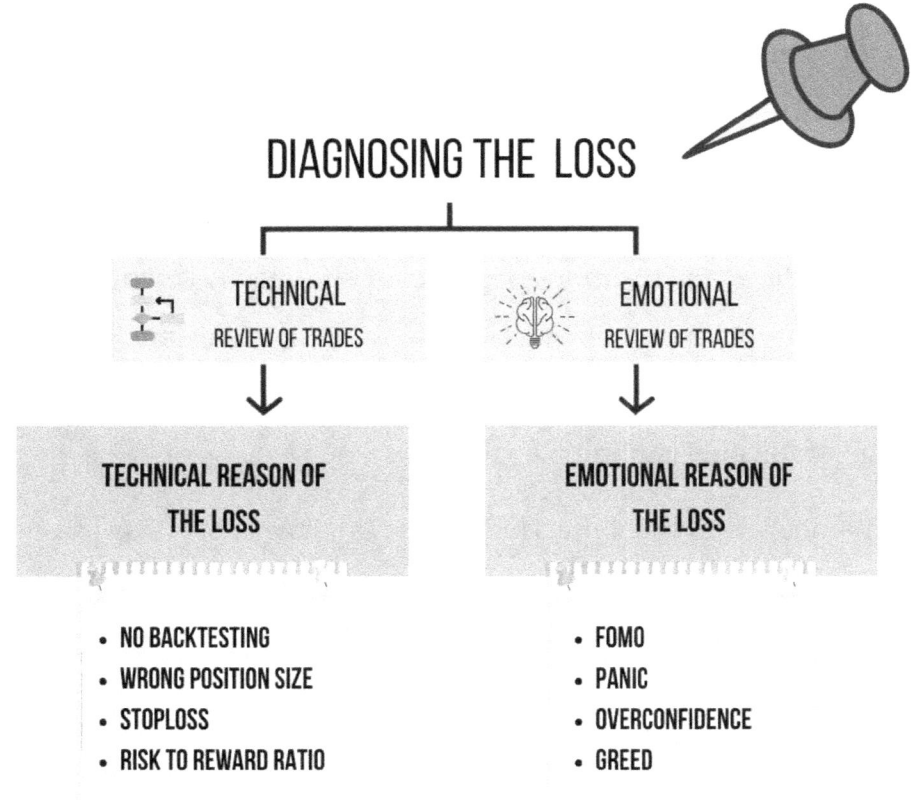

3. Do not Chase Losses:

When you have experienced a loss in trading, it is crucial to resist the urge to make a larger trade in an attempt to recover the lost money. This emotional response is driven by a desire to fix what seems like a mistake, and it often leads to impulsive decision-making.

Each trade is distinct, with its own set of goals, market conditions, and intended outcomes. It's essential to treat each trade independently, just like rolling a dice. The outcome of one roll doesn't influence the outcome of the next, and similarly, the result of one trade shouldn't dictate the size or approach of the next.

Making larger trades to recover losses can magnify the risks and potentially lead to more significant financial setbacks. It is important to approach each trade with a clear and objective mindset, considering the unique factors at play and adhering to your established trading plan.

Remember, emotional reactions in the aftermath of a loss can cloud judgment. Taking the time to assess and understand the specific conditions of each trade, rather than reacting impulsively, contributes to a more disciplined and strategic approach to trading.

4. Practise Response to Losing:

Responding to losses in trading requires a compassionate and constructive mindset. Even if you have made a mistake or encountered a loss, it's important to be gentle with yourself. Instead of dwelling on the error, focus on acknowledging it and extracting valuable lessons.

By adopting this mentality, you cultivate a healthier approach to risk evaluation. Rather than placing blame or dwelling on past errors, you become more adept at learning from experiences. This shift in perspective allows you to avoid repeating the same mistakes, ultimately safeguarding your trading account from unnecessary risks.

Remember, every trader encounters losses, and they are an inherent part of the learning process. Embracing a mindset of self-compassion and a commitment to continuous improvement enables you to navigate the challenges of trading more effectively. It empowers you to evolve and refine your strategies, contributing to long-term success in the stock market.

CHAPTER 9

OVERCONFIDENCE BIAS

Trading the markets requires confidence, which you may not have initially. You will experience defeats and setbacks in the trading industry, and the only way to get back up and fight back is to maintain unwavering confidence. However, it takes time to develop true, unshakeable trust in your trading ability.

It's essential to encounter a range of market circumstances and discover which trading tactics perform well in specific situations. This process takes more than a few months to complete. According to numerous trading professionals, it takes several years of trading experience to accumulate enough knowledge to instill true confidence. Novice traders, in the meantime, need to strike a balance between being overconfident and not having enough confidence.

A lot of inexperienced traders fail to learn from their errors. They keep an eye on the fluctuations in the markets and see how their account balance changes. They trade in markets that are unfavorable to their strategies and they don't choose high-probability situations. They make costly errors as a result of overusing their trading expertise. It is advisable to exercise caution, particularly following an unplanned winning run when you can experience euphoria due to an unexpected windfall. You will be more likely to take chances in such situations because you would think that you are only risking the "house's money." However, you should safeguard your wins because they belong to you, regardless of how you got them.

There are two kinds of overconfidence in trading:

- Prediction overconfidence
- Certainty overconfidence

Prediction overconfidence

The too-narrow confidence intervals that traders assign to their predictions are an indicator of the prediction overconfidence bias.

An example of this is when "experts" try to forecast precise price targets.

We frequently notice in the headlines that certain celebrities, analysts, or banks set absurd price targets or estimates. Simply put, forecasting with this level of accuracy is not feasible. Nobody will be able to predict with any degree of accuracy the precise price that a certain stock will reach in a given amount of days, not even skilled traders. They can only get a sense of the direction and some idea of magnitude.

That's overconfidence in predictions, or most of the time, it's just making things up to get attention.

Certainty overconfidence

Traders who exhibit certainty overconfidence bias are overly confident in their assessments.

Even with a strong system, you are only 60–70% certain when trading professionally, which is sufficient to turn a profit over the long term.

However, amateurs who see the identical trade become 90–100% confident that it will be a profitable trade. Because of this overconfidence bias, novice traders become blind to the possibility of a loss and believe that every trade they make is a "sure-win" trade. When a trade doesn't perform as expected, they may be shocked or disappointed. They also take on bigger risks, take bigger positions, and lack a stop loss or backup plan because of this.

Strategies for Handling Success Effectively:

1. Maintain a Disciplined Approach:

What to Do:

Stick to your trading plan and follow the strategies that keep your risks in check, even when things are going well.

Example:

Let's say you've had some successful trades. Now, it's crucial not to stray from your well-planned trading strategy. Stick to the limits you set for how much risk you are willing to take, and resist making quick decisions. Keeping discipline, which means sticking to your established ways of doing things, is the key to lasting success. Remember, just because things are going well doesn't mean you should ditch your structured approach. By staying disciplined, you make sure your success continues, and each trade fits your goals and how much risk you can handle.

2. Conduct a Post-Success Analysis:

What to Do:

Take a good look at what made you successful in trading.

Example:

Imagine you've been making money with your trades recently. It's important to figure out what exactly worked well. Take a close look at the strategies or decisions that helped you succeed. This detailed look gives you important insights into how you trade. By understanding what made you successful, you can improve and strengthen your good practices. This self-awareness is a powerful tool. it lets you use successful strategies again, adjust them to fit the changing market, and make your overall trading skills better.

Post-Success Analysis Assessment for Traders:

Q1: What specific strategies contributed to your recent success?

Interpretation:

- Identify the specific trading strategies that led to success.
- Assess the effectiveness and consistency of these strategies.

- Determine if the success was due to a particular market condition or a versatile strategy.
- Consider whether adjustments are needed for different market scenarios.

Q2: How well did you adhere to risk management rules during profitable trades?

Interpretation:

- Evaluate the degree of adherence to predetermined risk management rules.
- Calculate the average risk-reward ratio for profitable trades.
- Assess the impact of risk management on overall profitability.
- Consider if adjustments to risk management strategies are necessary for future trades.

Q3: Were your market analyses accurate, and did any unique insights play a crucial role?

Interpretation:

- Compare the accuracy of market analyses to actual market movements.
- Identify the tools or methodologies used for market analysis.
- Evaluate the role of unique insights or external factors in decision-making.

- Determine if there are opportunities to refine market analysis techniques.

Q4: How did emotions influence your decision-making during successful trades?

Interpretation:

- Reflect on emotional states during successful trades.
- Identify instances where emotions may have impacted decision-making.
- Consider strategies to maintain objectivity and discipline in future trades.
- Explore emotional management techniques to mitigate biases.

Q5: What areas for improvement and ongoing learning can you identify despite recent success?

Interpretation

- Acknowledge gaps in knowledge or skills despite success.
- Prioritize areas for ongoing learning and skill enhancement.
- Explore new resources, training programs, or mentors to further develop trading skills.
- Create a plan for continuous improvement based on identified areas.

Q6: How do you balance your perspective by reviewing both successful and losing trades?

Interpretation:

- Compare the analysis of successful and losing trades.
- Extract lessons from both types of trades, emphasizing the importance of learning from failures.
- Ensure insights from losing trades contribute to ongoing improvement.
- Use a balanced perspective to refine strategies and decision-making processes.

Q7: Have your long-term trading goals evolved based on recent successes?

Interpretation:

- Assess if recent success has influenced or altered long-term goals.
- Ensure that goals remain realistic, aligned with risk tolerance, and achievable.
- Consider adjustments to a long-term strategy based on evolving objectives.

Q8: How diversified is your trading portfolio, and how does diversification reduce risk?

Interpretation:

- Review the composition of the trading portfolio in terms of asset classes and instruments.
- Assess the degree of diversification and its impact on risk reduction.
- Identify opportunities for further diversification or rebalancing.

Q9: How often do you schedule assessments to review and adjust your trading strategies?

Interpretation:

- Evaluate the effectiveness of the current assessment schedule.
- Consider increasing or decreasing the frequency based on market dynamics and personal availability.
- Ensure that assessments lead to actionable adjustments in trading strategies.
- Maintain a proactive approach to staying adaptive in a dynamic market environment.

Consolidate findings from each question to develop an action plan. Implement changes in strategies, risk management, and continuous learning based on the analysis to maintain and enhance trading performance. Regularly revisit these questions to adapt to evolving market conditions and personal development needs. The goal is to foster a disciplined and reflective approach, sustaining success without succumbing to overconfidence.

3. Set New Goals:

What to Do:

Use the energy from your recent success to set new goals that are doable.

Example:

Think about hitting a big profit goal in your trading. Instead of just celebrating, use this success to set new targets for getting even better. This active way of thinking helps you keep growing and avoids getting too comfortable. By giving yourself challenges with goals that are both realistic and a bit ambitious, you stay excited and focused on improving your skills. This cycle of achieving goals and setting new ones becomes a powerful force pushing you to make steady progress in your trading journey.

Avoiding the Traps of Overconfidence:

Stay Humble:

Impact:

If you've been successful for a while, you might start feeling overly sure of yourself and make riskier decisions.

Example:

Picture a situation where you've been making money for a long time, making you think you can predict what the market will do. Confidence is good, but being too sure of yourself can make you take risky actions. It's important to stay humble because the market can be unpredictable. Recognizing that things can be uncertain helps you avoid the problems that come with being too confident. This humility acts like a shield, making sure your decisions are careful, well-thought-out, and in line with your overall risk management plan.

Regularly Assess and Adjust Strategies:

What to Do:

Keep checking and changing your trading plans to match how the market is changing.

Example:

A routine assessment of your strategies ensures they remain aligned with the current market environment. For instance, if you primarily rely on trend-following strategies, shifts in market sentiment or increased volatility might require adjustments. This adaptability safeguards your strategies against becoming outdated, helping you navigate the ever-changing terrain of financial markets with resilience and effectiveness.

Here are the most important metrics you need to track to assess and evaluate your trading strategies.

Traders can easily track the performance of their trading strategies by regularly evaluating a few key metrics associated with them.

These include,

1. **Sharpe Ratio**
2. **Maximum Drawdown**
3. **Win Rate**
4. **Profit Factor**
5. **Average Trade**

Sharpe Ratio:

An investing strategy's risk-adjusted return is measured by the Sharpe Ratio. It is computed by deducting the expected return of the investment strategy from the risk-free rate of return, which is the return on government security, or G-sec in India, and dividing the result by the standard deviation of the strategy's returns.

The formula for the Sharpe Ratio is as follows:

Sharpe Ratio = (Rp - Rf) / σp

where:

Rp = average return of the investment

Rf = risk-free rate of return

σp = standard deviation of the investment's returns

A Sharpe Ratio of 1 or higher suggests that your portfolio is generating returns at a rate that is higher than the average risk-free asset, like a treasury bond. However, a Sharpe Ratio close to 0.5-0.6 is considered acceptable in most situations.

Maximum Drawdown:

A trading strategy's maximum loss from peak (highest portfolio value) to trough (lowest portfolio value) is measured by a risk metric called maximum drawdown. It is employed to assess a trading strategy's possible downside risk and to assist traders and investors in comprehending the strategy's past performance.

The formula that determines the maximum drawdown is

(Peak Value - Trough Value) / Peak Value is the maximum drawdown.

where "Trough Value" denotes the strategy's lowest value during that same period, and "Peak Value" denotes the trading strategy's maximum value during that same timeframe.

A lower maximum drawdown is typically regarded as preferable since it shows that there has been less downside risk to the investment or trading strategy.

Win Rate:

Win rate is a performance metric that measures the percentage of profitable trades relative to the total number of trades executed by a trading strategy. It is a measure of a trading strategy's ability to generate profitable trades and is often used to evaluate the strategy's historical performance.

The formula for the win rate is as follows:

Win Rate = (Number of Winning Trades / Total Number of Trades) * 100%

You should keep in mind that a high win rate alone does not guarantee a desirable trading strategy performance. It's important to also consider other performance metrics such as the average win size, average loss size, and risk-adjusted return.

In some cases, a lower win rate can be acceptable if the average win size is significantly larger than the average loss size. This is because a few large winning trades can offset many small losing trades, resulting in an overall profit for you.

Profit Factor:

Profit factor is a performance metric used in algorithmic trading to measure the ratio of gross profits to gross losses generated by a trading strategy. It is calculated by dividing the sum of gross profits by the sum of gross losses.

A profit factor of 1 means that the strategy is breakeven, as the sum of gross profits equals the sum of gross losses. A profit factor greater than 1 is generally considered to be good because it indicates that the trading strategy generates more profit than loss.

The profit factor is measured using the formula,

Profit Factor = Gross Profit / Gross Loss

where "Gross Profit" represents the total profit generated by profitable trades, and "Gross Loss" represents the total loss generated by losing trades.

Average Trade:

Average trade is a granular performance metric that measures the average profit or loss generated by each trade executed by an algo trading strategy. It is calculated by dividing the total profit or loss generated by the strategy by the number of trades executed.

Average trade is calculated using the formula,

Average Trade = Total Profit or Loss / Number of Trades

where "Total Profit or Loss" represents the sum of all profits or losses generated by the trading strategy, and "Number of Trades" represents the total number of trades executed by the strategy.

CHAPTER 10

SOCIAL MEDIA INFLUENCE

External influences, such as peer opinions and the pervasive nature of social media, can significantly impact the decision-making processes of traders. Recognizing these influences is crucial for maintaining autonomy and making decisions aligned with your individual trading goals.

Psychological Impact of Peer Pressure and Social Media:

Fear of Missing Out (FOMO) from Peers:

Imagine you're a trader witnessing a sudden surge in a specific stock that your peers are capitalizing on. Instead of succumbing to FOMO, stick to your researched investment strategy. Assess the fundamentals of the stock, potential risks, and whether it aligns with your overall portfolio. Resist the urge to deviate from your plan solely based on the fear of missing out on short-term gains.

By adhering to these principles, you can maintain a disciplined and rational approach, mitigating the negative impact of FOMO on your decision-making process.

Social Media Validation:

Focus on internal validation and personal growth rather than seeking external approval. Base decisions on your values, goals, and expertise rather than the reactions of others. Consider adjusting privacy settings on your social media accounts. Share accomplishments selectively and be mindful of the potential impact of public validation on your decision-making. Before sharing achievements, assess whether it's genuinely for self-expression or driven by the need for validation.

Being aware of your intentions can help you make more authentic decisions. Imagine you achieve a successful trade and feel the urge to share it on social media for validation. Instead, consider whether the decision to share is based on genuine enthusiasm or a desire for external approval. If it's the latter, reassess the motivation behind the decision and whether it aligns with your overall financial goals. By prioritizing internal validation, adjusting privacy settings, and evaluating your intentions, you can make decisions that are more aligned with your personal values and financial objectives, rather than being swayed by the desire for external validation on social media.

Strategies for Maintaining Independence:

1. Trading Manifesto:

A trading manifesto is a personal document that outlines your trading principles, goals, and commitment to disciplined trading. It serves as a guide for decision-making and helps maintain focus during trading sessions.

Here is an example of my trading manifesto that will help you create your own.

Manifesto -

In my trading journey, I abide by a steadfast Trading Manifesto that acts as my guiding compass in the ever-changing landscape of financial markets. Grounded in principles of discipline, patience, and adaptability, I navigate both prosperous and challenging market conditions. My primary goal is to attain consistent profitability, accompanied by secondary objectives of effective risk management, continuous learning, and portfolio diversification. Prioritizing risk management techniques, such as setting stop-loss orders and diversifying my portfolio, is paramount to safeguarding my capital. I am committed to continuous learning, engaging with the trading community, and maintaining emotional discipline by taking breaks during stressful periods and journaling my emotions. With a well-defined trading system integrating technical and fundamental analysis, I diligently follow my system, adjusting it only after thorough analysis and reflection. Regular reviews and adaptation of strategies based on market dynamics underscore my commitment to long-term success. Recognizing the value of community, I actively engage with fellow traders to share insights and contribute to a collaborative trading environment.

This Trading Manifesto is crucial for guiding my actions and decisions as a trader. It serves as a compass, helping me navigate the dynamic and often unpredictable world of financial markets. By outlining core principles, setting clear goals, and emphasizing essential aspects like risk management, continuous learning, and emotional discipline, the manifesto provides a structured and disciplined approach to trading. It acts as a constant reminder of my commitment to these principles, ensuring that I stay focused on my objectives, adapt to market changes, and maintain a resilient mindset. Regularly reviewing and adapting the manifesto allows me to learn from experiences, refine strategies, and contribute to a supportive trading community.

2. Silent Trading Sessions:

Silent trading sessions involve designated periods where traders disconnect from external influences, including social media and news alerts. This fosters focused analysis and trading execution without external influences.

Schedule your entire trading session. During this time turn off notifications, avoid checking social media, and focus solely on market analysis and execution. Some apps help you focus better by starting focus sessions and disabling all notifications. Focus To-Do is one app that helped me to focus by using time-blocking sessions.

3. Customized Information Filters:

Curating a list of trusted financial news sources and tailoring social media feeds helps minimize noise and ensures access to valuable insights.

Identify reputable financial news sources. Create a list of these sources and adjust their social media feeds to prioritize accounts that provide high-quality, relevant market information.

4. Implement Focus/ Rhythm Music:

Structured work sessions with focus music help traders concentrate on their trading activities without distractions, enhancing overall productivity.

Assign yourself a specific trading-related task, such as analyzing a set of charts or reviewing their trading journal, and complete it during a focused work session.

Use focus music in the background to take your productivity and focus to the next level. This music can also be used while you are actively trading.

There is no other app that comes close to providing focused music than **Brain.Fm**. Brain.fm's focus music is made to help you work better, by blending into the background so you can focus distraction-free, all while stimulating the brain with gentle rhythmic pulses in the music that supports sustained attention. Brain.fm's functional music is designed from the bottom up to affect your brain and optimize your performance.

5. Screentime Management:

Developing screentime management strategies is essential for maintaining a healthy balance between trading and personal life, preventing burnout.

Track your screen time during trading hours for a week. Based on the data, identify areas for improvement and implement strategies to reduce unnecessary screen time. Strategies that can be used are using a downtime feature on your phone or creating a time limit on your social media apps, so you get less external influence while trading.

CHAPTER 11

MINDFULNESS

Mindfulness involves being fully present and aware of the current moment, free from distractions and emotional turbulence. In trading, cultivating mindfulness is invaluable for making rational decisions, managing stress, and fostering a disciplined approach. Trading can be an extremely demanding profession that requires a high level of focus. Sticking to the system is not the only thing effective traders must do. Another crucial skill that professional traders must have is the capacity to shut out unimportant ideas and concentrate only on their work. And a lot of traders decide to engage in mindfulness and meditation exercises to achieve this.

Benefits of Mindfulness in Trading:

Enhanced Focus:

Mindfulness sharpens concentration, leading to improved decision-making in trading. During intense trading sessions, the ability to maintain focus on market trends, signals, and crucial information becomes more accessible through mindfulness practices.

By cultivating mindfulness, traders can reduce distractions, stay present in the moment, and enhance their ability to make informed decisions. This heightened focus is instrumental in navigating the dynamic and fast-paced nature of financial markets, contributing to more effective and strategic trading outcomes.

Emotional Regulation:

Mindfulness aids in managing emotions, and fostering emotional resilience in the face of market uncertainties. In the context of unexpected market fluctuations, maintaining emotional regulation is crucial. Mindfulness practices provide traders with the tools to observe and manage their emotional responses in real time. Instead of succumbing to impulsive reactions driven by fear or anxiety, mindful traders can respond thoughtfully and make decisions based on a clearer, calmer mindset. This emotional regulation contributes to more stable and rational decision-making, even in challenging market conditions.

Practical Mindfulness Exercises for Traders:

1. Meditation Exercises:

Basic trading meditation

Anyone can do a simple form of meditation. This is the basic meditation for traders. You will see the difference if you are consistent in doing this for 5 days.

- Sit in a comfortable place with your back straightened out. It can be on the floor, against the wall, or chair.
- Breathe deeply and steadily through your nose alone and with your eyes closed. Using your mouth to breathe can activate a flight reaction, such as when you're running from danger.

- Concentrate on your breath without thinking about any other thing. You can count up to five in your head as you inhale and exhale each time to make your breathing even. You can try and imagine that there's an empty white movie screen standing in front. This will ensure you're relaxed and your thoughts are out of your mind.
- Do this for only 5 minutes. You can use a timer with a gentle alert tone to notify you.
- Before opening your eyes, take the last deep breath in while visualizing yourself in a calm and collected state. Exhale slowly before standing up and going about your day.

Transcendental meditation

This is another popular type of meditation that you have probably heard of. The simplicity of this meditation and the fact that it isn't tied to a lifestyle or religion are some of the reasons why it has become so popular. It is also very simple to practice.

Here are the steps to perform simple transcendental meditation:

So the first thing that you want to do is find a spot where you can sit down for five or ten minutes in your house and somewhere that you know you won't be distracted.

1. You can sit cross-legged on the floor, you can sit on a chair you can sit on the couch, whatever is comfortable for you. It doesn't matter.

2. Next, sit comfortably and then close your eyes. The first thing that you want to do is just take a couple of deep breaths to calm your mind and center yourself. So for me, I normally take three deep breaths, inhaling as deep as I can holding for a second and then exhaling.

3. And then once you've done that you want to perform a mindful body scan. A body scan is just taking a mental note of how your body is feeling. So scanning from head to toe seeing if there are any aches or pains or even if there are any feelings or emotions that are coming up. And the important thing is that we're just kind of taking note of how we're feeling. We're not judging in it anyway and we're just seeing how we feel at this stage. So if you have identified any painful emotions or physical sensations in the body, now's the time to take a couple of minutes just to focus on those sensations. Don't judge them. Just sit with them for a couple of minutes.

4. And then after this stage, it's time to introduce the mantra into the practice. So the mantra that I was taught is super simple, and it's just "OM". And what we want to do is repeat that mantra gently and silently in our minds and you almost want to have it pulsating on its own. So you're not controlling it. You're not focusing all your attention on it. it's just they're running in the background and what you'll find is that after a minute or so your mind might start to wander from that mantra and that's perfectly okay. A big part of TM is noticing when your mind has actually left the mantra and is trapped in thoughts and then gently bringing the mind back to the mantra. And through a meditation session, you might do that five, 10, 15 times and that's normal. The goal is not to stop thoughts but just to observe when you're lost in thoughts and then to come back to the mantra.

5. In the last couple of minutes of the meditation, you want to let go of the mantra and just sit in silence. And hopefully, if you've done this technique correctly you'll feel a lot calmer. Your mind will feel still and you should have fewer thoughts. And it's an awesome feeling.

6. And then once you've done that then you can just bring your attention to the body, feeling those bodily sensations. Wriggle your fingers and then slowly open your eyes and re-introduce yourself back into the world.

Qi Gong

This meditation practice is a good alternative for people who don't like sitting still. It's different from the conventional kind of meditation, but it also provides similar benefits. The main idea behind this meditation practice is that you're cultivating and redistributing the energy in your body. You have to move and breathe in a way that you're more centered.

2. Observing Thoughts Without Attachment:

Notice your thoughts without judgment. As market conditions evolve, take a moment to observe your thoughts about potential outcomes without attaching emotions to them. Acknowledge the presence of thoughts without immediately labeling them as positive or negative. This practice fosters objectivity in decision-making by creating a mental space where you can assess information more impartially.

By cultivating this non-judgmental awareness of your thoughts, you can develop a more resilient and composed mindset, enabling you to make decisions based on a clearer understanding of the situation rather than being overly influenced by emotions.

3. Progressive Muscle Relaxation:

Tense and then relax each muscle group. Start with your toes, tensing the muscles for a few seconds, and then release. Move progressively through the body, focusing on each muscle group. This technique helps release physical tension that may accumulate during intense trading sessions. By incorporating progressive muscle relaxation, traders can alleviate stress and maintain a more relaxed state, enhancing overall well-being. The physical release of tension can contribute to better emotional regulation and decision-making, as it allows traders to approach challenges with a clearer and calmer mindset.

4. Daily Reflection and Gratitude:

Reflect on daily trading experiences. End each trading day by taking a few minutes to acknowledge both challenges and successes. Reflect on the lessons learned from the day's experiences, whether positive or challenging. Express gratitude for the insights gained and the growth opportunities. This practice fosters a positive mindset by cultivating gratitude, which is essential for maintaining emotional well-being in the face of the uncertainties inherent in trading. By consistently incorporating daily reflection and gratitude into your routine, you can build resilience and approach each trading day with a more balanced and optimistic outlook.

Here is a template for daily gratitude and reflection.

Date: [Insert Date]

1. Morning Reflection:

Today's Market Outlook: [Summary of your expectations for the trading day]

Positive Affirmation: [Choose a positive statement to set the tone for the day]

2. Gratitude List:

List three things related to trading that you're grateful for today. This could include successful trades, learning opportunities, supportive community, etc.

[Gratitude item 1]

[Gratitude item 2]

[Gratitude item 3]

3. Lessons Learned:

Reflect on any lessons or insights gained from yesterday's trading. This could be a successful strategy, a mistake to avoid, or a new piece of market information.

4. Positive Trading Moments:

Recall and jot down any positive moments or achievements during your trading session today.

5. Challenges Faced:

Identify any challenges or obstacles encountered during your trading day. Note how you can learn and grow from these experiences.

6. Evening Reflection:

Today's Achievements: List at least three things you accomplished today in your trading journey.

Gratitude Recap: Reflect on the gratitude items from the morning. How did they positively impact your day?

7. Evening Visualization:

Visualize successful and positive trading experiences for tomorrow. Imagine yourself making informed decisions and navigating the market with confidence.

8. Daily Affirmation:

Choose or create a positive affirmation related to trading or personal development to carry with you into the next day.

Closing Thoughts:

Write a summary of your overall feelings and experiences related to trading today. End on a positive note, expressing gratitude for the opportunities and lessons.

[Your Name]

Sign

Feel free to customize this template based on your preferences and trading style. Consistently maintaining a gratitude journal can contribute to a positive mindset and improved emotional well-being, both of which are valuable assets in the world of trading.

It's a Marathon not a Sprint.

Congratulations on arriving at the final chapter, marking the culmination of our transformative guide to mastering trading psychology. Throughout this journey, you have delved into the intricate interplay between psychological factors and trading success, navigating challenges to traders and embracing a practical, step-by-step approach.

As you move forward, consider this not as the end but as a transition to a new phase of your trading journey. Cultivate a mindset of continuous learning, understanding that the dynamic world of trading requires adaptability and resilience. Recognize mindfulness as a lifelong skill, integrating exercises into your daily routine for clarity and emotional balance. Seek collaboration and support from peers, sharing experiences, strategies, and feedback to enhance your trading acumen.

Your journey in trading is an ongoing evolution. Reflect on how you've grown as a trader and let these insights guide your future decisions. Remember, trading is not just about making profits, it's a continual journey of self-discovery and refinement.

I extend my heartfelt gratitude for accompanying me on this comprehensive journey. Your commitment to mastering trading psychology is commendable. Stay connected with our trading community for additional resources, updates, and ongoing support. As you venture into the exciting world of trading, may each decision be informed, each challenge an opportunity, and each trade a step toward mastery.

Wishing you abundant success and fulfillment in your trading journey. Farewell for now, until we meet again on the shared path of continuous improvement and trading mastery.

About the Author

Pranam Ghagare

Pranam is a dedicated trader, NISM certified, and the founder of TrendWisdom. Featured on Investing.com as an author, Pranam has over five years of full-time trading experience and a unique perspective that goes beyond conventional approaches. Driven by a deep passion for the stock market, Pranam dropped out of architecture studies to pursue trading. With a growing community of over 10,000 followers on social media, he is committed to coaching and empowering individuals through his company, TrendWisdom. Having trained more than 2900 people, Pranam shares his insights aiming to see traders win and positively impact their lives and families.

www.ingramcontent.com/pod-product-compliance
Lightning Source LLC
Chambersburg PA
CBHW071205290526
45796CB00008B/156